basic gardening skills

basic gardening skills

jane mcmorland hunter
and chris kelly

Launched in 1938, the **teach yourself** series grew rapidly in response to the world's wartime needs. Loved and trusted by over 50 million readers, the series has continued to respond to society's changing interests and passions and now, 70 years on, includes over 500 titles, from Arabic and Beekeeping to Yoga and Zulu. What would you like to learn?

be where you want to be with **teach yourself**

Orders: please contact Bookpoint Ltd, 130 Milton Park, Abingdon, Oxon OX14 4SB. Telephone: +44 (0) 1235 827720. Fax: +44 (0) 1235 400454. Lines are open 09.00–17.00, Monday to Saturday, with a 24-hour message answering service. You can also order through our website www.hoddereducation.co.uk

British Library Cataloguing in Publication Data: a catalogue record for this title is available from the British Library.

Library of Congress Catalog Card Number: on file.

First published in UK 2008 by Hodder Education, part of Hachette Livre UK, 338 Euston Road, London, NW1 3BH.

This edition published 2008.

The **teach yourself** name is a registered trade mark of Hodder Headline.

Typeset by Transet Limited, Coventry, England.
Printed in Great Britain for Hodder Education, an Hachette Livre UK Company, 338 Euston Road, London NW1 3BH, by Cox & Wyman Ltd, Reading, Berkshire.

Impression number 10 9 8 7 6 5 4 3 2 1
Year 2012 2011 2010 2009 2008

contents

plant lists and tables

Lists

Tables

acknowledgements

Firstly, I must thank Hare, John and my parents for encouraging me to garden and allowing me free rein in their various properties.

Sue Gibb has been a fount of horticultural knowledge. Any remaining mistakes are mine but without her there would have been many more.

Donald Cameron and Fraser McKenzie provided a sunny terrace to write on and some much needed computer expertise. Lily Piachaud, David Piachaud and Paul Honor also rescued us on the computer front at various stages.

Barry Delves and Valerie Scriven have provided great encouragement along the way.

Finally, I must thank Eric Treuille, Sally Hughes, Camille Rope, Charmain Ponnuthurai, Lindy Ford, Marilou Amante and Shelley McGlashan for being so tolerant of the gardener in their midst.

Jane McMorland Hunter

There are far too many individuals to whom I am indebted to single anyone out in particular. However, I must pay tribute to the many wonderful gardens that have inspired me and especially those at West Dean in Sussex.

Chris Kelly

We are obviously very grateful to each other – writing this book has been great fun.

Our agent, Teresa Chris, has been a constant source of support and enthusiasm and at Hodder, Victoria Roddam and Jenny Organ have made the writing of this book a pleasure.

dedication

To Louy and Janice, with love from us both.

introduction

Gardening is one of the most pleasurable and satisfying activities. It has been practised by humans since ancient times and can now be traced to almost all regions of the world. At first it may seem like an intimidating secret society for people with green fingers; in fact an enormous amount of gardening simply relies on common sense and the rest is easily mastered. Many of the techniques have evolved gradually over hundreds of years but increasingly, in the twenty-first century, we are faced with a new set of factors that need to be taken into account.

This book assumes no prior knowledge of gardening and explains clearly in straightforward steps what you need to know and do to create and maintain the garden that suits you. It is also designed to be used as a reference book for more experienced gardeners who want information on a particular subject.

To the beginner, gardening can appear to be a minefield of Latin names and unintelligible terms. In fact you probably already know more than you think. Many people can recognize the flowers indicated by the words *Fuchsia*, *Delphinium* and *Iris*, and it only takes common sense to translate *Lilium* and *Rosa* into lilies and roses. Indeed, the popular television programmes normally use both Latin and English names when describing a plant. Libraries may be filled with books on subjects such as pruning, but all this really involves is cutting off dead or unwanted parts of a plant. Obviously there are methods and suitable times for pruning that you need to learn about but again they are simple enough to master. A large number of gardening books are available: many appear terrifyingly technical and others simply seem to consist of beautiful but unattainable images. Don't be put off by this – much of the technical information you will never need and it will only take a little time and effort to produce a beautiful garden of your own.

One of the greatest attractions of gardening is that it can be enjoyed by anyone, regardless of their age, fitness, income or training. You don't even need to own the garden, and some of the best work is done on rented allotments (and they're now very fashionable!). You don't need to be a botanical expert or wildly creative and, unless you want to, you don't even need to spend that much time on your garden. Many plants take moments to put in the soil and many can cost little or nothing, but they will give you months or even years of colour and interest in return. In an increasingly hectic and stressful world it is very satisfying to get so much for so little. While your gardening will obviously be restricted by the available space, you will be surprised how much you can achieve even with a couple of window boxes.

While a great deal of gardening is common sense, there are a number of worthwhile rules and tricks that make it far easier and more rewarding. Of course, you can gain your experience through trial and error, but this may cost you money and effort as well as wasted time. Even worse, it can be very disheartening. Spending money on a plant that needs bright sunlight and then trying to grow it in deep shade is not likely to be successful, and it only takes a little research (sometimes just reading the label) to site plants where they will be happy. Some groundwork beforehand is far better than watching your plant die, slowly. One of the aims of this book is to provide you with the knowledge based on experience and mistakes (ours!) that will save you from wasting your time and money.

Regardless of the causes, it is an inescapable fact that our climate is changing. How quickly and to what extent it will change is for science to debate, but already our gardens are subject to phenomena such as drought and flooding to an unprecedented extent. Many of the traditional ways of gardening are becoming irrelevant or even harmful to the environment. It is important to take these changes into account when you garden and to try and work with nature rather than against it.

Another inescapable fact is that human actions affect the planet. Again, the level and consequences of these actions are the subject of great debate, but whereas advocates of organic and sustainable gardening were once regarded as cranks, their methods are now recognized by many as the best way. Gardening organically does not mean you have to wear a sackcloth shirt and use a compost toilet. Equally gardening sustainably does not mean you have to use old cans as containers unless you want to. What it does mean is using methods that leave the environment as it was, or in even better condition. This is surprisingly easy and often more successful than the intensive, chemical-based approach of the last century. Gardens are not natural phenomena but rather result, like farms, from our shaping of nature. Yet the closer we can work with nature, the better they will work and the better off we will be. On a basic level this simply means choosing plants that will be happy in the conditions you have to offer and then looking after them as naturally as possible. Using chemicals to solve a problem is rarely a long-term solution as this often creates a wider imbalance in the garden. It is preferable and easier to create a situation where the problems do not arise in the first place.

This book is laid out so that you can easily find the answers to any questions you may have. Chapter 01 is aimed at finding out what you want from your garden. It is important to remember you are more likely to succeed at something you enjoy and that gardening should be fun. Chapter 02 shows you how to assess what you already have in your garden. It is vital to work with your soil and climatic conditions, etc; otherwise your garden will become a battleground through a war with nature. This means doing things as obvious as improving your soil rather than trying to change it, growing plants that actually suit your prevailing conditions, and putting the pond in the wettest bit of the garden! Sticking to the basic ground rules makes gardening easier and your garden look much better.

Chapter 03 shows how you can put your ideas into practice and create the garden you want. Chapter 04 looks at the details of patios and courtyards, either as part of a larger garden or as an entire small garden. Chapter 05 covers the plants you might want to use; it explains the different groups and suggests how to use them in the garden. Throughout the book there are lists of recommended plants – these are only a small selection to give you ideas. Many plants qualify for more than one list, for example, if you need a climber for a shady wall it is worth looking at the climbers list as well as the shady list.

Chapter 06 explains the tools you might need and Chapter 07 covers all the techniques for looking after your garden, taking you from a bare patch of rubble to a beautiful setting. Maintained sustainably, gardens offer us huge benefits: they look beautiful, give pleasure and help redress the imbalances in our lives that modern lifestyles have created. In the case of gardening, it is possible to help the planet and yourself at the same time.

Chapters 08 and 09 cover the specific subjects of containers and growing food. All gardens benefit from a few containers and you will see from Chapter 09 how simple and satisfying it is to grow at least some of your own food. Chapter 10 provides a season-by-season list to help remind you what to do when. These chapters are followed by a glossary explaining all the terms we have used. Finally, there is a list of useful books, websites and other resources in the 'Taking it further' section to help and inspire you on your gardening adventures. Please remember that the idea of this book is not only to get you gardening sustainably, but also to *enjoy* your gardening.

Latin names explained

Although the Latin names of plants may seem very complicated, there is actually an easy logic to them and the great advantage of using them is that they are part of a universal plant labelling system. This system was devised by Carl Linnaeus (a Swedish botanist who is regarded as the founder of modern botany) in 1753 at a time when Latin was the language of science and was also the only international language.

Plants are grouped together in a 'genus', which is usually the first name on the label and is in italics with a capital or capitals throughout, for example, *Clematis*. Genera are brought together in larger groups still (families), but these are not so important from a horticultural point of view and the family is rarely given in plant lists or on labels.

The individual plants within the genus are called 'species' and this is also written in italics but without a capital. This part of the plant's name is often descriptive, for example, *Clematis montana* (from mountains). It can be a useful indicator of the sort of conditions the plant would thrive in, such as *maritima* (by the sea), *nivali* (growing near snow) or *himalayensis* (from the Himalayas). If several plants of the same genus are listed together, the genus is represented by its first letter, for example, *Clematis alpina*, *C. montana*, *C. cirrhosa*, etc.

If the species needs to be broken down further, the subspecies (subsp./ssp.), variety (var.) or form (f.) follows the species name. These are also usually written in italics without a capital, for example, *Clematis montana* var. *rubens*.

Cultivars are cultivated varieties that differ horticulturally but not botanically – colour or the breeder's name being the most common features. The name is not given in Latin (apart from some older cultivars); it is printed in normal type and has single quotation marks and capitals, for example, *Clematis macropetala* 'Markham's Pink'.

A hybrid is a plant that is the offspring of two different plants. If it is a mixture of two species of the same genus, this is indicated by an 'x' in roman type after the genus, for example, *Clematis* x *durandii*. The two species are not necessarily both listed. If the hybrid genus involves the interbreeding of two genera the 'x' appears at the front, for example, x *Cupressocyparis*.

In the text plants are referred to by their common names, snapdragon for example, and their Latin names are used only to describe a particular species or variety, for example, *Buddleja globosa* or *B. davidii* 'Black Knight'.

Throughout the book you will find lists of recommended plants for the various conditions you may encounter in your garden. These are listed alphabetically according to the Latin names, with any common names in brackets. Each plant has a brief description to give you an idea of its main features. If a particular species is listed it means that plant is especially suitable. If we simply name a genus, you can assume that most plants within that genus will be suitable. Always check the details of any species; *Acer pseudoplatanus* and *A. palmatum* may sound similar but there is a 20 m (85 ft) difference in their heights! Bear in mind that the lists provide only a small selection; there will be many more plants that you could use.

what sort of gardener are you?

In this chapter you will learn:

- **how to get what you want from your garden**
- **how to create a garden that will suit you and your family**
- **how to garden sustainably and enjoyably.**

In order to enjoy gardening you need first to spend a little time working out what you want to get out of it. Imagine how you would like your garden to look and then balance that against the practicalities of your way of life. The amount of time and money you want to invest in the garden is obviously a key factor, as is the condition, site and aspect of the garden itself. Finally, you need to consider how much physical labour you can or want to put into gardening.

You may wish to spend most of your free time sitting in the garden or you may prefer to be more active. Gardens can be easily designed to suit all these requirements but a little thought is needed before you rush out and buy a mass of plants. You need to consider when you will primarily use the garden and how regularly you will be able to water it. If you go away every weekend and for long periods in the summer, you will either need to arrange for someone to come in and water your plants or choose specimens that are tough enough to survive on their own. Vegetables and annuals have to achieve a lot of growth in a short space of time and therefore need constant care and watering, whereas many perennials, roses and shrubs can survive for long periods without water once they are established.

The type of garden you choose to create will also depend on how long you are going to live there and how quickly you want results. If it is a garden that comes with a rented flat, a few containers may suffice. These have the advantage that you can move them around according to the seasons and, perhaps more importantly, take them with you when you go. If you are prepared to let your garden mature slowly, you can grow plants from seed and gradually add to what is already there. If you inherit an established garden, it is always advisable to leave as much as possible (within reason!) for at least one season so you can see what you have. It is very easy to dig up perennials inadvertently when they have died back for the winter.

If you have a completely blank canvas, such as with a new house, you will have more scope as to what you can do, but you need to plan more carefully. Tempting as it is to create an 'instant garden', try not to be in too much of a hurry to do things so that you can avoid costly and time-consuming mistakes.

Many gardens have to cater for the requirements of the whole family, and for this each person needs to be taken into consideration. Safety is of paramount importance if you have small children, so you need to be aware of the potential dangers of features such as ponds and the growing of poisonous plants. An area of rough lawn can make a good play area, and at a later stage sandpits and plain areas of grass can be converted into ponds and flowerbeds. There is no point in making your children hate the garden by imposing too many restrictions on them. It is better to organize at least part of it around their needs and gradually convert it to what you want as they grow up. Many children become keen gardeners if they are given their own area of ground and a little encouragement. Some may overcome their hatred of eating vegetables if they are involved in the growing process. You also need to take into consideration your own age and mobility and that of the rest of your family or any regular visitors. Too many changes of level can make getting around the garden difficult for people who are elderly or have disabilities, while wide paths and raised beds make access easier for wheelchair users.

It is also worth considering *how* you will garden. Using chemicals may seem like an easy option, but avoiding them will make your garden a healthier place and, in turn, will actually make gardening simpler. It will also help the environment as a whole. Your individual plot may only be small, but the thousands of gardens throughout the world cover a huge area. Garden sustainably, reusing or recycling where you can, and you will make the earth a better place at no great cost to your garden or yourself. In fact, the closer you can work with nature, the more successful your garden will be.

The style of garden you have will depend on your taste and circumstances and may change as you go along. It is only at flower shows and on television makeovers that a garden is 'finished'; in reality your garden will be subtly changing all the time. Decide roughly what you want and go from there. At this stage you are probably not sure what you want, but that is one of the charms of gardening – you can do almost whatever you like. Even if all you wish to do is sit in a deckchair and simply *look* at your low-maintenance garden, there is nothing to stop you doing just that, and by doing so you will have achieved what you want from your garden.

02 assessing your plot

In this chapter you will learn:

- **to make the most of your existing garden**
- **what are the factors which will affect your garden**
- **how to work out what climate and soil you have**
- **how to deal with perceived problems like shady, dry, damp or windy sites.**

Introduction

You may have a rough idea of how you want your garden to look but, before you put these ideas into practice, you need to take account of the site and any conditions affecting the garden. This means looking at the area as a whole and finding out what advantages or constraints you may need to consider. It is possible to modify the natural factors affecting your garden, but it is always easier to work within the existing conditions rather than trying to fight them.

This chapter shows you the main things to take into consideration and how to work with them. Each section will show you how to recognize the various characteristics of your garden, explain the causes of the natural factors, and show you how you may be able to modify these if necessary.

- Consider what you want.
- Think about what you have.
- Match up the two.

The existing garden

Firstly, look very carefully at your garden and see what is already in it. (If it is an area of uncultivated mud and rubble this will obviously not take very long!) Take time to consider the merits of everything in the garden.

1 Look at the plants and see how well they are doing. Don't rip up something that you don't particularly like the look of without thinking why it is there and whether anything else would do as well.
2 Look at the features in the garden and, again, wait before moving or removing them. At first sight the patio may not seem to be in exactly the right place but it may be perfectly positioned to catch the sun or shade at a particular time of day. (Equally it could simply have been put there by the builder of the house with no real thought, in which case you may need to modify it.) Once you understand why something is where it is you can make an informed decision about whether to keep it or not.
3 You need to consider what surrounds your garden. A belt of trees will provide shelter but may also cast shade over your garden.

4 You need to take the aspect into account, that is, which way your garden faces. This will have a great influence on which plants will do well. Work out where north is and consider each side of the garden in turn. In the northern hemisphere a south-facing side will get the sun from mid-morning to mid-afternoon and is, in many ways, the easiest site to cultivate. West-facing sides get the afternoon and evening sun, which is also good, but in Britain they can be windy as they face in the direction of the prevailing wind. East-facing sides get the morning sun and, although this may look adequate, it actually does not do much good horticulturally because early in the day the sun has very little warmth and after a frosty night this tiny amount of heat can actually harm plants – it causes them to thaw out too fast, damaging shoots and buds. North-facing sides have little or no sun, and only shade-tolerant plants will flourish here. However, these areas often have the advantage of being sheltered.

The climate in and around your garden

Two types of climate may affect your garden – the macroclimate of the whole area in which you live and microclimates that may affect particular areas within the garden.

Macroclimates

It is fairly clear that the weather has become much more unpredictable since global warming and climate change have increased. What the causes are and how fast any changes will occur is uncertain, but it is already having an impact on our gardens and, in particular, on the types of plants we can grow. Rising temperatures mean we can grow a wider range of tender plants, but mild, wet winters may not suit plants which need a cold, dormant period. The best solution is to work out roughly what sort of climate you are most likely to experience and then base your plans around that.

- Is the area windy or do you live by the sea (in which case the wind will be salt-laden and you will need to choose salt-tolerant plants as windbreaks)?
- How much rain do you get and does it rain steadily or do you have dry periods interspersed with thunderstorms?

- Do you regularly have heavy frosts or are your winters mild and damp?
- How much, if any, snow do you expect?
- Do you have long or short summers?

All these considerations are general and may vary from year to year, but they will give you an idea of the type of plants which are likely to thrive in your garden. Your garden will be more successful if you use plants that are indigenous or that come from an area with a roughly similar climate.

Microclimates

Microclimates may affect the particular area in which you live or particular areas within your garden. Some examples you may need to consider are:

- gardens within cities tend to be warmer than those in the surrounding countryside as buildings absorb heat by day and release it at night
- gardens right on the coast will have a more moderate climate than those inland as the sea will reduce temperature fluctuations, but they may be subject to strong winds
- valleys may be more sheltered than the surrounding hills but they may equally contain frost pockets which can be very cold and damp.

Microclimates will exist within your garden even if it is tiny.

- The side of your garden that faces the south (in the northern hemisphere) will be warm and sunny with little moisture. The opposite side that faces north will be shady and considerably cooler.
- One side of your garden may be much drier if it is in the rain shadow of the building. This means the wind will sweep any rain over or around the building, leaving an area behind the obstacle where little or no rain falls.
- The amount of sun your garden gets in the different seasons will depend directly on tall obstacles in and around it. Buildings, trees or hills may block the sun all year round or only in winter when the sun is lower in the sky.
- Walls or hedges along a flowerbed may provide shelter but they will probably leach much of the water out of the soil. Fences will not do this as, unlike bricks, they do not absorb water.

- Certain areas of your garden may be windier than others. Tall buildings closely spaced together can cause wind tunnels – the wind is channelled through the narrow gap and becomes much stronger. Balconies raised above ground can also be windy as they usually have little or no protection.

There are means of modifying many of these conditions, but it is worth being aware of what you have right at the start.

The type of soil

It may seem surprising but the soil is probably the single most important part of your garden. If you have good soil your plants will grow more strongly and be able to withstand other privations such as too much wind or you forgetting to water them. This section shows you how to work out the main characteristics of your soil and Chapter 07 shows you how to get it into tip-top condition. Most soil is made up of the bedrock beneath it, hummus (organic matter), water and air. Of these it is the bedrock that will largely determine the soil's characteristics. It is perfectly possible (and often desirable) to modify soil but you can never really successfully totally change it as the earth is always developing from the bedrock.

All soil has a pH level which is a number between 1 and 14 that indicates how acid or alkaline your soil is. Pure water is 7, anything above this is alkaline and anything below is acid. Many plants do not mind what level they grow in and many people never test their pH levels. However, certain plants have specific requirements and will struggle or even die if these levels are ignored. Testing your soil is easy using a kit that can be bought at any garden centre, and it will give you an idea of your soil's pH level. Test several areas of your garden as you may find the pH levels vary quite considerably in different areas. Most plants will be fine between 5.5 and 7.5, but in many ways a slightly acidic soil (5.5 to 6.5) is best as acid-loving plants tend to be fussier. As a general rule, soil is tending to become more acid due to industrialization and the resulting 'acid rain'.

You also need to know what type of soil you have as this will largely determine its structure which, in turn, will determine how well it retains water and nutrients. It is usually quite simple to assess the main soil component by seeing how quickly it drains and by feeling it. Dig a hole roughly 30 cm/1 ft deep, fill it with water and watch how quickly it drains away. If it has drained away after five minutes you have free-draining soil; if it is still there half an hour later your soil is slow to drain. Take a small piece of soil and squeeze it in your hands; depending on its make-up it may feel gritty or form a smooth ball. The main types of soil are described below, each with their own advantages and disadvantages, but remember that most garden soils will be made up of a mixture of different types.

Chalk

This is easily recognizable as it has small particles of white chalk in it. It drains rapidly and is alkaline. It can be improved by digging in organic matter.

Clay

This is also easily to recognize as it feels slightly sticky when wet and can be rolled into a ball. It is slow to warm up in spring and has a tendency to become waterlogged, but it can also dry out and crack during droughts. It may feel cold and heavy and be hard to dig when wet, but it holds nutrients well and the texture can be improved by adding organic matter and grit.

Limestone

This soil is normally full of rocks, which increase as you dig down where the bedrock breaks up without difficulty. It drains rapidly and is alkaline, but not usually to such an extreme extent as chalk. As with chalk it will be improved with the addition of organic matter.

Sand

Sandy soils are light in colour and will feel rough and crumbly. They warm up quickly in spring but drain rapidly, and nutrients tend to be washed away and need replacing regularly. It is usually acid. Mixing in organic matter and adding mulch on top will help considerably.

Peat

This is a dark, acidic soil that develops slowly over time and can hold a huge amount of water by absorbing it like a sponge. Unless you live on the edge of a peat bog you are unlikely to have a significant amount in your soil. It can be made more workable with additions of lime, grit, sand or ash.

Loam

Having this type of soil has been described as the gardening equivalent of being born with a silver spoon in your mouth. It is a mixture of sand and clay with a good percentage of hummus and a neutral pH. Sadly it does not often occur naturally in gardens but, with a little effort, you can aim most soils in this direction.

Hummus

Hummus is not a type of soil but, ideally, it is present in the top layer. It largely consists of organic matter and makes soil rich, dark and crumbly. It provides fertility, helps retain moisture and allows the passage of air through the soil, all of which are vital. In cultivated soil it breaks down quickly and needs to be regularly replaced by adding home-made compost, leaf mould or well-rotted manure.

New build and stony soil

If your soil contains a lot of stones, you need to work out where they have come from. New build is not strictly a type of soil but it is frequently found in the 'gardens' of newly-built houses. Compacted builders' rubble and mud with some cheap soil on top might be a more accurate if somewhat cynical description. This can be improved by removing the rubbish and the largest stones, and digging in compost or well-rotted manure as explained in Chapter 07. This may seem tedious when all you want to do is make your garden look attractive but it really is worth doing right at the start. Nothing, not even rough grass, will survive long when growing in earth and stones that have been squashed by heavy machinery and have no proper structure.

If your stones are coming up from the bedrock, you will need to work with them rather than trying to fight the conditions. They may be inconvenient when you are digging, but there are some advantages: stones retain heat well and will prevent the soil becoming cold at night. The soil will also warm up more quickly in spring. In heavy soils stones help drainage and, although they may make light soils drain too fast, surface stones will slow the rate of evaporation. Dig in plenty of organic matter to help the structure of the soil and only clear the stones if they are hindering the plants. If you are planting a lawn from scratch or making a seedbed you will need to clear the stones, and it will make digging easier if you clear vegetable beds but otherwise it is really not worth worrying too much.

Shady gardens

Shade in a garden is often regarded as a difficult problem to be overcome but, in many ways, it is actually an advantage. Shade means that the plants are protected from the burning heat of the midday sun in summer, they warm up gently after frosty nights and are therefore less prone to damaged buds in early spring, and less water is lost through evaporation. Shade only becomes a problem if the light levels are very low or if insufficient water reaches the soil.

You need to work out what density of shade you have, when it occurs and what the soil is like in the area. The permanent shade created by a tall building is different to that caused by an open-branched deciduous tree. The type of shade (see list below) and soil together will determine whether you are dealing with damp or dry conditions.

- Deep shade.
- Dry shade.
- Moist shade.
- Dappled shade.
- Daily and seasonal variations.

Deep shade

In gardening terms, 'deep shade' means in the shade all day and at all times of the year. This type of shade is common in city gardens where surrounding walls and tall buildings will mean that part of almost every garden is in deep shade. Side passages and light wells are particularly common examples. In larger gardens, evergreen trees can cause areas of deep shade. You may find this makes the soil particularly dry as the barriers blocking the sun may also block any rain. On the other hand, depending on the type of soil, you may end up with an exceptionally damp area as no sun reaches it to dry it out.

There are a considerable number of plants which have adapted to deep shade and would indeed die if planted in harsh, bright sunlight. Many, such as *Mahonia*, have large, thin dark green leaves perfectly suited to making the most of the low light levels. Many ferns have finely dissected and sometimes hairy leaves which trap moisture and reduce transpiration. Most shade-tolerant plants have widely spreading roots to make the most of any water and this is why it is so important to prepare the soil well. You need to be aware that some plant groups simply don't like deep shade.

- Of the herbs, only mint, chives and parsley will thrive.
- Grasses are fine in partial shade but don't like deep shade. Most ferns are all right though.
- Grey- and silver-leaved plants need good levels of sunshine to grow well although *Anaphalis triplinervis* (pearl everlasting) will be happy as long as your soil is reasonably damp.
- Morello cherries (*Prunus cerasus*) are the only fruit trees that do well in shade, but with beautiful spring blossom and delicious fruit what more could you ask?
- Variegated or pale-leaved plants are a good way of creating the illusion of light in a dark area, but if the light levels are very low the leaves may revert to dark green. The ivy *Hedera helix* 'Buttercup' has bright yellow leaves in sunlight but if planted in deep shade they will gradually turn green.

By and large pastel colours look better in shade than very bright ones. Deep blues and maroons can look wonderful but vivid reds and oranges tend to look harsh and garish. Exactly the same goes for walls and ground cover. Cream or white walls will instantly make an enclosed space feel lighter. Similarly, pale paving or gravel is usually a better choice than dark bricks or stone on the ground.

Another trick is to replace tall fences with trellis and climbing plants. This can let in a surprising amount of dappled sunlight and still give you a reasonable degree of privacy. The best solution is often to have a solid barrier at the base (say 1.3–1.6 m/4–5 ft) with trellis on top. Judicious pruning of trees may also let in more light, but if you are dealing with a large, established tree it is always worth asking the advice of a qualified tree surgeon.

When choosing plants, try to go for seasonal interest and colour variations as well as an ability to thrive in shade. All mahonia do well in shade but the leaves of *M. aquifolium* turn a beautiful reddish purple in autumn and *M.* x *media* 'Charity' has clear yellow flowers from autumn right through winter. You will quickly find that there are masses of wonderful plants which thrive in shade. Below is a selection to get you started.

Plants for deep shade

These plants will do well in anything from dappled to deep shade. Unless specified, they prefer reasonably well-drained soil that does not dry out too much in summer.

Anemone hupehensis, *A.* x *hybrida* (Japanese anemone) – tall perennial with clumps of attractive leaves and pink or white flowers in late summer.

Aquilegia – dainty perennial with flowers that look like tiny birds on tall stems in early to midsummer. Tolerates any soil.

Dicentra spectabilis (Bleeding heart) – clump-forming perennial with arching rows of truly beautiful heart-shaped pink or white flowers in early summer. Tolerates any soil.

Fuchsia – shrub of varying size with masses of pendant flowers in summer and autumn. Many of the flowers are bicoloured, mixing reds, pinks, purples and white. Choose hardy varieties unless your garden is very sheltered.

Hydrangea – rounded deciduous shrub with mop heads of flowers which fade attractively in autumn. The colour will depend on your soil, acid giving shades of turquoise and blue and alkaline tending towards pink.

Impatiens (Busy Lizzie) – an annual that is often sneered at as it is used so often in institutional planting schemes. The more unusual double varieties are much more attractive, forming flower-covered hummocks in reds, pinks and white from midsummer until the first frost.

Monarda (Bergamot) – tall perennial with big shaggy flowers from midsummer to early autumn and aromatic greeny-grey leaves.

Rosa (Rose) – a surprising number of roses do well in shade.

Sarcococca (Christmas box) – evergreen shrub with very fragrant flowers in winter. The tiny white flowers are followed by small, glossy black fruits. Tolerates any soil.

Variegated or bright foliage for shade

These plants will keep a certain level of variegation in shade, but they all do best given some light.

Astrantia major 'Sunningdale Variegated' – perennial with deeply lobed leaves edged in creamy white. In summer green, pink or magenta flowers rise above the foliage, each with a little ruff of pale pink bracts.

Berberis thunbergii 'Rose Glow' – spiny deciduous shrub with small leaves that start purply-red and fade to pink as the summer progresses. Tiny primrose yellow flowers in spring are followed by red berries.

Hosta – many hostas have striking leaves and most do well in shade. Many have small, bell-shaped flowers in shades of lavender in summer but there will be fewer flowers if the plant is in deep shade.

Ilex (Holly) – many hollies are variegated but you will need plants of both sexes if you want berries.

Pachysandra terminalis 'Variegata' – low-growing, evergreen perennial which is useful for ground cover. The mid-green leaves have creamy-white edges, and in early spring there are spiky white flowers followed by oval white fruits.

Weigela florida 'Variegata' – bushy deciduous shrub with white-edged, grey-green leaves. Funnel-shaped, rose pink flowers in spring and summer.

Dry shade

An area of dry shade needs a little care before you plant anything unless you want to spend all your time remembering to water it regularly. Firstly, you need to work out why it is so dry:

- The area may be in a rain shadow.
- The soil may drain too quickly so any rain soaks away before it can do any good.
- If the area is exposed it may be dried out by the wind. Surprising as it may seem, strong winds will dry plants and soil faster than direct sunlight.

You probably can't remove the obstacle causing the rain shadow, but you can improve the soil to enable it to hold more water. To lessen the power of the wind you want to slow it down rather than stop it totally with a solid barrier that would probably make matters worse. The section on windy conditions (see page 29) shows you how to do this. Mulching once you have planted will reduce evaporation. You will have then created a more sheltered environment which will lose less water and generally be more conducive to plant growth.

Plants for dry shade

These plants will tolerate moderate levels of shade and like soil that remains reasonably dry at all times (see also page 22).

Anemone nemorosa – low-growing perennial with deeply divided leaves forming a carpet. Large, blue star-shaped flowers from spring to summer.

Geranium (Cranesbill) – varied group of perennials that usually forms attractive clumps. The leaves are often interesting shapes and some change colour in autumn. The flowers are white, pink, purple or blue and some varieties repeat-flower throughout the summer.

Kerria japonica – deciduous shrub with tall arching stems and rich yellow flowers in early summer. *K. j.* 'Pleniflora' has pompom-shaped flowers which continue intermittently throughout the summer.

Meconopsis cambrica (Welsh poppy) – small perennial with yellow and orange cup-shaped flowers throughout summer.

Ribes sanguineum (Flowering currant) – deciduous shrub with slightly hairy leaves and red or pink flowers in spring, followed by small black fruits. *R. s.* 'Brocklebankii' has pale yellow leaves and does well in shade.

Moist shade

This is a far easier combination to deal with because lots of plants like a cool, damp, shady environment. Dig in organic matter to ensure your soil has all the nutrients it needs and dig in sand or grit if it is very sticky. As with all soils, it is worth mulching every year as this will enrich the soil and suppress any weeds.

Plants for moist shade

These plants will tolerate moderate levels of shade and like soil that remains damp at all times (see also page 25).

Aconitum (Monkshood) – tall perennial with spires of deep blue, hooded flowers in autumn.

Anaphalis triplinervis (Pearl everlasting) – this is the only silver-leaved plant that will thrive in shade. It is a clump-forming perennial with domed heads of little white flowers in summer.

Astrantia – clump-forming perennial with flowers on tall stems. The flowers are usually pinky-white and are surrounded by a collar of greeny-pink papery bracts.

Crinodendron hookeriana (Lantern tree) – a beautiful evergreen shrub with red lantern-like flowers in late spring and early summer.

Meconopsis betonicifolia (Blue poppy) – the blue poppy can be difficult to grow unless you meet its requirements exactly – moist but well-drained, rich acid soil and dappled shade sheltered from cold winds. That said, the amazing turquoise blue of the flowers makes it well worth trying.

Polygonatum (Solomon's seal) – perennial with small bell-like flowers hanging from arching stems in late spring and early summer.

Dappled shade

This is most commonly found beneath deciduous trees, and the level of shade can vary considerably depending on the type of tree and the time of year.

1 Check the canopy isn't so solid that the area is plunged into deep shade in summer. Trees such as maples (*Acer*) create a more open covering than magnolias, which can be almost solid. It is often possible to prune a tree so it lets more light through but it is always best to get a qualified tree surgeon to do this.
2 Be aware that the trees are liable to leach much of the water and nutrients out of the soil. This can be remedied by mulching each year with garden compost or well-rotted manure. Be careful when digging in organic matter as many tree roots are near the surface and you may damage them.

There is a wide range of plants you can use in these conditions. Spring bulbs will benefit from the sun that the bare branches allow through and the protection they provide over winter. Most variegated and pale-leaved plants will flourish, making the area appear even lighter. If the canopy is solid in summer, grow more shade-tolerant varieties as they will survive better and won't mind the winter sun that does reach them. Any woodland or jungle plants will do well so you can create almost any type of garden you want. Below is a selection of plants that will happily settle at the base of deciduous trees or large shrubs and give you colour and interest throughout the year.

Plants for beneath deciduous trees and shrubs

Any of the plants in the deep shade or dry shade section lists (see pages 13 and 15) above will survive but the following are particularly adept at fitting in between the roots of trees.

Erythronium (Dog's-tooth violet) – small clump-forming perennial. The flowers hang downwards from short upright stems and have distinctive recurved petals. They come in all shades of pink, purple, yellow and white and last from mid-spring to summer.

Polygonatum (Solomon's seal) – perennial with arching stems from which white bell-like flowers hang in late spring and early summer.

Primula – primrose-polyanthus primulas are a varied group of clump-forming perennials with flowers in winter and spring. They come in a huge variety of colours and are often grown as biennials for short-term displays.

Pulmonaria – low-growing perennial with attractively mottled hairy leaves. Small spring flowers in shades of pink, blue, purple or all three.

Viola odorata (Sweet violet) – small semi-evergreen perennial with dainty, sweetly-scented blue or white flowers in late winter or early spring.

Daily and seasonal variations

The level of shade in your garden may vary quite dramatically according to the season or the time of day. A flowerbed may get sun first thing in the morning and then be in shade for the rest of the day. Equally, an area which is shady all winter may receive direct light in summer when the sun is higher in the sky. By looking at your garden throughout the year you will find that a clear pattern of the movement of light and shade emerges. You don't need to be particularly exact or scientific about this; you will soon be aware of the sun's path by simply sitting in the garden for morning coffee or afternoon tea. The main points to bear in mind are as follows:

- Early morning sun may warm plants up too quickly after a cold night and damage the buds of spring-flowering plants. Camellias are particularly susceptible to this.
- Areas that receive midday sun in summer need to be planted with sun-loving plants even if they are in shade for most of the winter. Ensure the ground doesn't become too damp in winter as most sun-loving plants hate the combination of wet and cold.
- Remember when positioning your patio that you are unlikely to eat out much in winter so it doesn't matter if the light levels drop then and the area is in shade. Also bear in mind that while a sunny breakfast may be lovely, by lunchtime you are likely to want some protection from the sun. You can always sit under a parasol but the dappled shade of a gently rustling tree would be much more attractive.
- Choose your plants so they will get the conditions they like for most of the year. Most perennials do not mind if they are in shade when they are dormant during the winter. Equally, sun-loving annuals can be planted in an area that loses its sun in the winter as they probably will not survive the winter anyway. You do need to be careful that winter-flowering bulbs and shrubs get enough light, so plant them taking the winter conditions into account, not those at midsummer.

Drought conditions

Until the last few years nearly anyone in Britain would have been laughed at if they said their garden regularly suffered from drought. Certainly some areas, such as portions of East Anglia, experienced times of drought in some years but these were seen as one-offs rather than regular occurrences which needed a strategic response.

The causes of drought

Drought conditions in gardens occur for a number of reasons. Lack of rainfall is the most obvious, but the condition of the soil greatly influences any rain that does fall. Sun and wind will affect the rate at which water evaporates from the ground and is transpired by plants. Microclimates of dry areas may also occur in gardens where there are large trees, hedges and walls.

As a general rule, rain falls, sinks down into the soil, returns up through it and into the plants and is released into the atmosphere to fall again as rain in due course. Less water is lost in winter (many plants have fewer leaves and the sun is not as strong), allowing more to be stored in both plants and soil. This is why winter droughts are more serious in the long term than a dry summer. Equally, gentler rain during the night is more useful than a brief downpour on an otherwise sunny day.

Even if you live in an area with comparatively high rainfall, your garden can still have a microclimate of drought. Trees and hedges can suck up all the available water, creating dry zones around them. Walls and buildings make rain shadows, with the prevailing wind sweeping any rain over the obstacle and leaving an almost permanently dry area to one side. Brick walls make it worse by absorbing any water that does reach the soil.

Choose the right plants

While some plants can survive without soil, no plant can survive without water. Many desert plants have adapted so they can wait months or even years for rain, but this patience does not necessarily make them attractive specimens for a garden. Most ornamental garden plants need water on a slightly more frequent and regular basis. Most drought-tolerant plants tend to be just that, tolerant of drought if necessary.

You can modify conditions in your garden to a certain extent by improving the soil and by watering efficiently, but the most important thing is to choose the right plants. Many plants have adapted to deal with drought conditions and will thrive in your dry garden, looking beautiful and making your work much easier as they will need less looking after.

Features to look out for in drought-tolerant plants include the following:

- Plants with leaves that are very small (such as thyme) reduce the surface from which water is lost.
- Plants with leaves that are very thin (lavender and rosemary) limit the amount of water lost through transpiration.
- Plants with larger leaves, but with a covering of fine hairs, reduce water loss and trap any available moisture such as early morning dew. These hairs give many of the plants an attractively furry or downy appearance, for example, rabbits' ears (*Stachys byzantina*).

- Plants with silvery leaves, like sea holly (*Eryngium*) reflect the light, thus reducing heat and evaporation.
- Plants with a blue (glaucous) tinge to the leaves, as found on sedums, often have a waxy coating that will reduce heat and evaporation.
- Aromatic-leafed plants like myrtle (*Myrtus communis*) store water well because the oils that produce the scent also trap water in the leaves.
- Succulent plants, such as agave and sedum, store water efficiently in their thick sap.
- Plants with long taproots that go really deep into the soil reach water buried deep below the dry surface.
- Many of the bulbs which flower in spring or early summer (e.g. tulips and alliums) do so before the weather gets too hot and they then retreat underground where it's cooler. Some plants, such as irises, actually need their rhizomes (roots) to be baked in the sun in order to flower well the following year.

Put the plants in the right place

When choosing plants it is vitally important to consider whether your site is sunny, shady or a mixture of the two according to the sun's position during the day and throughout the seasons. While water will evaporate more slowly from a shady position, there may also be less of it in the first place if, for example, that shade is caused by a building or tree.

Improve the soil and drainage

By and large, soil is best improved by digging in plenty of organic matter. However, you have to be a little careful with drought-tolerant plants since many cannot cope with too rich a soil or waterlogging in wet periods and they become sappy and floppy as a result. Many drought-tolerant plants can't cope with really wet winters and many more die from sitting in soggy soil than from extremes of cold.

- In clay soil, grit and sand are better than organic matter such as compost since they break the soil up without over-enriching it.
- On fast-draining sand or chalk, organic matter will hold the soil together and is fairly safe since there are not many nutrients to start with. Good soil structure will encourage plants to develop deep roots and become less vulnerable to water shortages at surface level.

Water sensibly for drought conditions

The key points about watering are as follows:

- Water when you first plant something.
- Make sure the water doesn't drain away too quickly.
- Soak the ground thoroughly when you do water.
- Provide water at the times that plants need it most.
- Keep an eye on your plants (particularly containers) for signs of distress.

When you first plant anything you will always need to give it some water – no matter how drought tolerant it is.

For all plants, it is better to water thoroughly from time to time rather than frequently but inadequately. Watering is best done in the evening after the heat of the sun has passed and directly onto the root area. For individual trees or shrubs you can create a saucer in the earth around the plant to prevent water flowing away.

It is important to know when your plants need water. For example, for many flowering shrubs the first half of the summer is more important than the second while fruit trees have their greatest need around the time the fruits start to swell.

Many gardens are only affected by drought occasionally or for relatively short periods of time. In this case you can make sure your plants remain healthy by watering really thoroughly so the moisture seeps right down and encourages the roots away from the hot surface. Containers will need watering every day but more established plants growing directly in the soil shouldn't need water more than a couple of times a week. Keep an eye on any vulnerable plants and, since prevention is better than cure, aim to water before they wilt.

Once the soil is properly damp (right the way down, not just the top 1 cm/½ in), you can retain water there by mulching. For dry gardens, gravel is particularly appropriate since it prevents water evaporating, does not make the soil too rich, and looks good against the predominantly silver and blue foliage of drought-tolerant plants.

Finally, getting rid of weeds is important if water is in short supply since they will merely compete for what is there with your own, possibly more delicate, ornamentals.

Plants for dry conditions in sun or partial shade

Acanthus (Bear's breeches) – big perennial with tall spires of pink and white flowers in early summer. Impressive, spiny-edged leaves.

Alchemilla mollis (Lady's mantle) – low perennial with attractive leaves and delicate greeny-white flowers in summer.

Cotinus coggygaria (Smoke bush) – deciduous shrub turning brilliant orange or red in autumn. In summer, red flowers grow in fluffy panicles, giving the plant its name.

Echinops ritro (Globe thistle) – compact perennial with clumps of spiny leaves which are green above and felty-white below. Bright, metallic-blue flower balls on tall stems in summer.

Lunnaria annua (Honesty) – tall annual or biennial. Late spring flowers followed by flat silvery seed pods.

Sedum spectabile (Ice plant) – clump-forming deciduous perennial with glaucous leaves. Rounded heads of pink flowers in autumn. *S.* 'Herbstfruede' is tall and *S.* 'Ruby Glow' is shorter with dark flowers.

Stachys byzantina (Rabbits' ears) – mat-forming perennial with velvety-soft leaves. Woolly, purple flower spikes in summer.

Plants for shady drought conditions

(See also page 15.)

Brunnera macrophylla – perennial ground-cover plant with hairy leaves and small blue flowers in spring.

Cyclamen hederifolium – low-growing perennial. Pink autumn flowers followed by attractive leaves during winter.

Epimedium (Bishop's mitre) – low ground-cover perennial. Attractive leaves with pink, red or yellow flowers in spring and summer.

Helleborus foetidus (Stinking hellebore) – low-growing perennial. Green flowers with purple edges from winter to spring. Leaves stink if crushed but flowers are pleasantly scented.

Polygonatum (Solomon's seal) – perennial with small bell-like flowers hanging from arching stems in late spring and early summer.

Pulmonaria – low-growing perennial with clumps of hairy mottled leaves. Small spring flowers that can be purple, pink, blue or all three.

A number of ferns will thrive in deep shade, including most varieties of *Asplenium*, *Dryopteris* and *Polystichum*.

Plants for full sun and drought conditions

Most bulbs, grasses and herbs.

Abelia – evergreen or semi-evergreen shrub with glossy, dark green leaves and masses of small, tubular, pale pink flowers from midsummer to autumn.

Agapanthus (African blue lily) – perennial with wonderful star-bursts of flowers in mid- to late summer ranging from deep blue to white. Strap-like evergreen leaves.

Catanache caerulea – short-lived perennial with grassy leaves and pretty cornflower-like flowers in summer.

Eryngium (Sea holly) – striking perennial with spiny leaves in steely blues and silvers. Oval heads of tiny flowers rise up from spectacular bracts or base leaves.

Eschscholzia californica (Californian poppy) – annual with finely cut leaves and lots of single orange flowers in summer.

Gaura lindheimeri – short-lived airy perennial with grassy leaves and pink and white star-shaped flowers all through summer.

Linum (Flax) – ranging from annuals to small shrubs, most are deciduous and have pretty blue, white or yellow flowers in summer. *L. grandiflorum* is an annual and has flowers in shades of pink and crimson.

Papaver orientale (Oriental poppy) – perennial with delicate papery flowers in shades of red, orange, pink or white.

Potentilla – low-growing perennials and deciduous shrubs. The perennials have red, pink or yellow rose-like flowers surrounded by strawberry-shaped leaves. The shrubs make medium-size dense bushes with small, single or double flowers in the same colours as the perennials. Both flower from summer to autumn.

Scabiosa caucasica (Pincushion flower) – annuals and perennials bearing summer flowers in blue, white, yellow or pink with pincushion-like centres and delicate, papery surrounding petals.

Verbena bonariensis – tall, airy, tender perennial with dainty clusters of tiny purple flowers which float above the plants below.

Damp or flood-prone gardens

Damp soil can be divided into three main categories:

1. Soil that retains a high percentage of water and easily becomes waterlogged.
2. Soil that is permanently wet or boggy due to a constant supply from water such as an adjacent river or an underground stream.
3. Soil that is subjected to periodic flooding.

Each type of soil requires a slightly different treatment and will be home to slightly different plants. Of course, you may not be able to find out if your garden gets flooded until it is too late, but check for nearby streams or rivers and ask your neighbours. Most plants will survive a flash flood but you will need to choose more resistant plants if parts of your garden are regularly under water.

Making the most of damp soil

- Organic matter will improve the structure of the soil, allowing water to pass through and also creating air pockets that are vital to the health of the soil and any plants growing in it. Unless your soil is very compacted, do not dig too deeply as you may make matters worse by bringing soggy subsoil to the surface. About a spade's depth is absolutely fine in most cases.
- Surface mulch will improve the soil as it gradually breaks down. It will also hinder the growth of weeds. These tend to grow quickly in damp soil and, given half a chance, will take over at the expense of your less robust plants.
- When planting, dig wide shallow holes rather than deep ones. Ensure the base of the plant is, if anything, fractionally above ground level and then spread the roots out as much as possible. If you put your plant in so that it is below ground level, it will simply attract surrounding water and end up sitting in a puddle.

According to whether your site is sunny or shady, different plants will be suitable. Selections for both are given below.

Plants for a damp shady site

(See also page 15.)

Astilbe – clump-forming perennial with fluffy spires of tiny flowers in mid- to late summer. After the pink, red, purple or white flowers fade, the pale brown seed heads can remain intact until winter.

Corydalis flexuosa – low, clump-forming perennial with delicate ferny leaves and brilliant turquoise tubular flowers from late spring to summer.

Gentiana – autumn-flowering varieties of this perennial thrive in damp shade. *G. asclepiadea*, *G.* 'Inverleith', and *G.* x *macaulayi* 'Well's Variety' have attractive blue tubular flowers.

Phlox paniculata – perennial with clumps of lance-shaped leaves and dome-shaped clusters of sweetly scented flowers in summer and autumn. The flowers are red, blue, purple or white, often with contrasting centres.

Primula – all primulas will grow happily in damp shade. Polyanthus tend to form low clumps whereas the candelabras bear their flowers on taller stalks. They are perennials and many are evergreen.

Salix x *sepulcralis* 'Chrysocoma' (Weeping willow) – fast-growing, huge tree with long yellow shoots and lance-shaped leaves that hang to the ground.

Ferns: *Adiantum*, *Asplenium*, *Blechnum*, *Dryopteris*, *Osmunda*, *Polypodium*, *Polystichum*

Grasses: *Carex*, *Hakonechloa*, *Milium effusum*

Plants for a damp sunny site

Astrantia – clump-forming perennial with flowers on tall stems. The flowers are usually pinky-white and are surrounded by a collar of greeny-pink papery bracts.

Cornus (Dogwood) – deciduous shrubs with attractive summer flowers, brilliant winter stem colour or interesting foliage. *C. alba* has dark green leaves which turn purple in autumn, dropping to reveal bright crimson stems, *C. kuosa* var. *chinensis* has creamy-yellow flowers in summer, followed by red fruits and leaves in autumn.

Echinacea (Coneflower) – tall perennial with large daisy flowers in purple, pink or white in late summer and well into autumn.

Euphorbia – many euphorbias do well in damp sunny spots. *E. griffithii* has bright red or orange flowers in late spring. The leaves start red and gradually turn green. *E. palustris* is a clump-forming perennial with clusters of yellow flowers in spring and leaves which turn orange in autumn. *E. sikkimensis* has bright green leaves that are often tinged pink and form dense clumps with yellow flowers in late summer.

Helenium – clump-forming perennial with tall daisy-like flowers with raised velvety brown or yellow centres. The late summer flowers come in all shades of yellow, coppery orange and red.

Lysimachia – many varieties of this perennial make tall clumps with elegant flower spires. *L. clethroides* (Gooseneck loosestrife) has arched spires of tiny white flowers in late summer resembling a goose's neck.

Monarda (Bergamot) – tall perennial with aromatic foliage and wild flower heads throughout summer in shades of pink, lilac and crimson.

Boggy gardens

If your land runs alongside water or has an underground stream, it may be permanently marshy. Here you need to grow plants that like to have their roots in water all the time. These plants are often referred to as 'marginal' as they like their leaves dry and their roots wet. They will usually thrive in anything up to 15 cm/6 in of water.

This area would be an ideal place to create a water feature, particularly a wildlife pond which would benefit from a surrounding damp margin. As with most things, it is best to work within the constraints you have and in this case it is rarely worth trying to drain a permanently wet area.

Marginal plants

Any of the plants listed on page 25 and above will thrive in permanently moist soil at the edge of water. The following plants will thrive with their roots actually *in* the water.

Butomus umbellatus (Flowering rush) – perennial with rush-like twisted leaves which start purple and turn dark green. Pink flowers in late summer. Needs full sun.

Caltha palustris (Marsh marigold) – clump-forming perennial with cup-shaped buttercup-yellow flowers on tall stems in spring. Likes sun or part shade.

Iris – irises come in a large, slightly confusing range. The ones for this type of area include *I. laevitica* (Water iris), *I. pseudacorus* (Yellow flag iris), *I. versicolor* (Blue flag iris). They have upright strap-like leaves and flower in a variety of colours in early summer. Likes sun or part shade.

Juncus effusus 'Spiralis' (Corkscrew rush) – perennial with long, curly, grass-like stems along which there are small brown flowers in summer. Likes sun or part shade.

Schoenoplectus lacustris subsp. *tabernaemontani* 'Zebrinus' (Variegated club rush) – upright green stems with creamy-white bands and pale brown spikelets at the top in early summer. Worth growing despite the length of its name! Best in partial shade.

Typha (Bulrush) – perennial with tall, upright leaves and brown flower spikes which will form large dense clumps. *T. minima* is suitable for small ponds. Happy in sun or shade.

Zantedeschia aethiopica (Arum lily) – perennial with arrow-shaped green leaves and pure white flowers in early summer. Needs full sun.

Flood-prone gardens

Flooding is a much more serious and unpredictable problem that we are increasingly having to deal with as our climate becomes more uncertain. The amount of damage caused by flood water depends on the intensity of the flood itself and on how long it lasts.

- Flash floods are common in summer when the ground is dry and hard and unable to absorb the water from a sudden heavy downpour. They are becoming more common as front gardens are paved over to make way for cars and the water has nowhere to go. This sort of flooding rarely lasts more than a few hours, and although your plants may not like it, they are unlikely to suffer any lasting harm.
- Floods which occur because the ground is already saturated may last considerably longer. The main danger to plants here is that the air pockets in the soil will fill with water. Annuals, Mediterranean plants and most herbs are particularly vulnerable if the flooding lasts more than a couple of days.

- The deeper the water the more harmful it is as more leaves are submerged, effectively cutting off the plant's air supply.
- Fast-flowing water may undermine the roots of plants of all sizes. Wet soils lose the ability to hold together and may also be swept away by passing water.
- Moving flood water will probably deposit silt and other debris in your garden. The silt from the River Nile may have kept Egypt fertile but most of the stuff dumped on your plants by passing flood water will probably do much more harm than good.

If you know your garden, or part of it, floods regularly, it is worth taking a certain amount of evasive action to minimize any damage.

- Raised beds are a useful way of protecting tender plants if your flood water isn't too deep. They must have solid sides so the soil does not wash away, and be robust enough to withstand any flowing water. Bricks or thick planks are usually the best options.
- Berms or long earth mounds can be used to divert water on a large scale. It is usually worth getting professional advice for the exact size and position as you may make matters worse by channelling the water and giving it extra strength. You also need to give careful consideration regarding where the diverted water goes; you will not be popular if you simply divert it into your neighbour's garden.
- Dry stream beds can be used to accommodate extra water and carry it away. Again be careful of the siting so the water is carried away harmlessly.
- Water butts can hold a large amount of water that would otherwise drain into your garden. Try and position one at the base of every downpipe. These will reduce the risk of flooding and enable you to save the water for dry periods.
- Make the soil structure as good as possible so it drains well. Mulch every year to maintain this structure. In this way, the soil will hold together better even when wet. This will also help with alternating periods of wet and dry weather.
- Choose plants that are more tolerant of flooding. A selection is given on page 29.

If your garden is flooded there are a number of things you can do to minimize the damage and help it recover as quickly as possible.

- At first do nothing. You will cause more harm than good walking on flooded soil and until the water subsides there is no action you can take.
- Once the water has receded, put planks down to walk on so you do not compact the soil.
- Clear away any mud and debris as this will smother the plants. Rain may wash some of this away, but if it does not it is worth clearing the area with a hose. A little more water will do less harm than a thick layer of sludge.
- Do not walk on lawns until they have dried out. If you need to cross them, put down planks and remove them as soon as possible to allow air to reach the grass. Once it has dried, rake to remove any dead grass.
- Check any plants for structural damage and stake if necessary. With large trees it is worth asking a qualified tree surgeon to look at them as the plant may seem fine but it could be weakened to the point where it could fall at a later date.
- Be patient. Many plants may look dead but they will recover with time.

Flood-tolerant plants

Trees and shrubs: *Aronia* (Chokeberry), *Betula* (Birch), *Cydonia* (Quince), *Ginko biloba*, *Magnolia*, *Mespilus germanica* (Medlar), *Salix* (Willow), *Vinca* (Periwinkle)

Perennials: *Achillea*, *Campanula persicifolia*, *Cardamine pratensis* (Lady's smock), *Euphorbia palustris*, *Hemerocallis* (Daylily), *Hosta*, *Iris pseudacorus* (Yellow flag), *I. sibirica* (Flag iris), *Leucanthemum* x *superbum* (Shasta daisy), *Liatris* (Gayfeather), *Ligularia*, *Lobelia cardinalis*, *Lysimachia ciliata*, *Mimulus* (Monkey flower), *Miscanthus sinensis*, *Osmunda regalis* (Royal fern), *Panicum virgatum* (Switch grass), *Persicaria*, *Polemoniun* (Jacob's ladder)

Bulbs: *Fritillaria*, *Galanthus* (Snowdrop), *Leucojum vernum* (Snowflake), *Lilium* (Lily), *Scilla*

Windy conditions

All gardens need some wind to circulate the air in them, but there is a great difference between a gentle breeze and a strong gusting gale. Strong winds can do an enormous amount of damage and their strength needs to be reduced before they enter your garden.

The effects of wind in a garden

- Water loss is the single most important effect of wind on plants. Usually, water moves up through a plant at a slow steady pace. Strong winds will dry the leaves as soon as the water reaches them, faster than it can be replaced. Plants can appear to be suffering from drought even if the soil is damp. This is especially harmful in winter when the water may be frozen and trapped in the soil. Evergreens are particularly vulnerable and should be gently sprayed with water to keep them damp.
- Constant wind from a single direction can cause lopsided or stunted growth. Leaves and stems may be broken off and the growing tips on the exposed side are constantly pinched back. This is particularly noticeable on coastal sites where there is often a constant wind off the sea. Foliage and tips can also be damaged by being rubbed together.
- Wind reduces the temperature and can turn a cold day into a potentially harmful one for tender plants.

Situations where wind may be a problem

- All newly planted plants are at risk until they have established a good, firm root system. For trees and shrubs this usually means the first couple of years; for annuals it may be their whole life.
- New growth on an existing plant is usually delicate, especially spring buds.
- Gardens in built-up areas can suffer from strong winds which are channelled between buildings.
- Roof gardens and balconies tend to be exposed to stronger winds as they are high off the ground and do not usually have much protection.
- In large gardens, hillsides may be windy as the wind is channelled down the slope. When putting up a barrier, check that cold air will not be trapped at the bottom of the slope causing a frost pocket.
- Seaside gardens are a special case as here you will need plants that are both wind and salt tolerant. Any wind off the sea will probably be quite gentle, but it will be constant and salt-laden.

The solution to almost all of the above situations is to slow the wind down to a point where it does no damage. Unlike a lot of natural conditions in your garden, it is usually comparatively easy to lessen the effects of strong winds. The important thing to remember is that you want to filter the wind rather than totally block its path. If you put a solid barrier up, the wind will simply go over or around it, eddying and gusting on the far side and causing more harm. If the wind has to negotiate a partial obstacle, it will be slowed down and become less damaging. Think of walking into a wood on a windy day. There is no solid barrier but the wind is effectively lessened by the trees until the air is quite still.

Protecting the garden

- If you have a large garden, a couple of loosely structured layers make the best windbreaks. This could be a line of deciduous trees with a mixed hedge in front or openwork fencing with climbers and a selection of robust shrubs in front.
- In a small garden, trellis with climbing plants is often the best solution as trees and hedges take up a lot of room and leach the surrounding soil of nutrients and water. Climbers, such as certain roses, ivy (*Hedera*) and trumpet vine (*Campsis radicans*), will fill out the trellis, look attractive and not mind the wind. The batons need to be 2 cm by 3 cm/¾ in by 1¼ in thick in order to be strong enough to withstand the constant buffeting they will receive.

Any windbreak needs to be large enough to protect your garden. As a rough guide, a windbreak will protect an area of garden equal to twice its height, i.e. if your hedge is 2 m/6 ft tall it will protect 4 m/12 ft of garden. It will give some protection for up to five times its height but you have to bear in mind that the level of protection will decrease as you get further from the windbreak.

If your garden is not enclosed at either end of the barrier, bear in mind that some wind will sweep around either end with renewed vigour. The solution here is to either make the barrier wider than it needs to be or continue it around at an angle so the wind is deflected away from the garden.

Protection within the garden

- Young plants should be supported with stakes or a temporary structure to filter the wind. Your windbreak will be vulnerable when first planted, but you can protect it with a fence of loosely woven hurdles which can be removed after a couple of years when the plants are firmly established.

- On a smaller scale, tall tough plants can be used to protect smaller ones. Box edging around flowerbeds is good, as are step-over fruit trees. Taller plants or climbers can be trained against trellis or openwork screens to provide protection at the back of an exposed bed.
- Winter winds tend to be more damaging, so in autumn make sure all your climbers are well tied into their supports. Also cut back any open-shaped shrubs which could be vulnerable. Roses and buddleja are typical of the shrubs that can get blown about and damaged. Cut away about a third of the total amount you would normally cut away in spring. This will protect the plant against the worst of the winter winds and you can finish pruning it at the usual time in spring.
- Lastly, mulch any bare soil. This protective layer will prevent water from evaporating and will also stop the soil being blown away. Garden compost, well-rotted manure or mushroom compost are all good; hay, straw or cocoa shells are too light and are liable to be blown away.

All the plants listed below have adaptations which mean they do not mind being subjected to constant wind and will act as protectors for your more delicate plants.

Wind-tolerant plants

Amelanchier – deciduous shrubs or small trees with pendant clusters of pretty white flowers in spring. Fruits follow, which can be eaten when cooked, and the leaves then turn brilliant orange and red in autumn.

Buddleja globosa (Orange ball tree) – semi-evergreen bushy shrub with orange ball-shaped flowers in summer.

Centranthus ruber (Red valerian) – clump-forming perennial with clusters of tiny flowers from late spring right through summer. The fragrant flowers are white or shades of pink and crimson.

Eryngium (Sea holly) – metallic-blue thistle-like perennial with spiny leaves and cone-shaped flowers in summer.

Escallonia – evergreen shrub with small, glossy green leaves and an abundance of tiny pink, white or red flowers in summer.

Festuca glauca (Blue fescue) – tufty, evergreen, perennial grass with striking blue leaves.

Lupinus arboreus (Tree lupin) – bushy semi-evergreen shrub with palm-like grey-green leaves. In late spring and summer there are spires of fragrant pale yellow and occasionally blue flowers.

Molinia caerulea (Purple moor grass) – tufty perennial grass with purple bases to the green leaves and purple spikelets at the top of the stems from spring to autumn.

Philadelphus (Mock orange) – bushy deciduous shrub with very fragrant white flowers in summer. The cup-shaped flowers can be single or double and may be tinged with pink.

Rosa (Rose) – many old or wild roses are tough enough to withstand strong winds. *R. banksiae*, *R. glauca*, *R. pimpinellifolia*, *R. rugosa*.

Rosmarinus (Rosemary) – evergreen shrub with fragrant greeny-grey foliage and little blue flowers in early summer.

Tamarix (Tamarisk) – deciduous shrub or small tree with feathery foliage and plumes of pink flowers in late spring or summer, depending on the variety.

designing the garden you want

In this chapter you will learn:

- **how to create a sense of privacy in any garden**
- **how you can still have a beautiful garden even if you do not have much time**
- **how to get what you want from your garden.**

Introduction

As explained in Chapter 01, there are many different ways of designing your garden and it is important that you choose the one that is right for you, your family and your lifestyle in general. Using your available resources (money, time, plot, strength and skills), you will want to make something that:

- is well built and safe – you don't, for example, want to have to rebuild features after a couple of years, let alone install paving that becomes dangerously slippery or build an unfenced swimming pool or water feature where small children may subsequently be playing
- does what you want – if you want to sunbathe by the house then it's not a good idea to build a patio in an area that is always shady or overlooked
- makes you happy – if you and anyone who uses your garden likes it and it doesn't annoy anyone else (for example, your neighbours – by stealing all their light) that is all that really matters. People's tastes will always differ and fashions change over the years, but choosing the things and plants you like, successfully put together in the way you like, will give you the best opportunity to enjoy your garden and your gardening. What William Morris said of houses could equally well apply to gardens: 'Have nothing in your house that you do not know to be useful or believe to be beautiful.'
- possibly, but more likely nowadays, is environmentally friendly and encourages biodiversity.

Even if you take on an established garden, it is still worth taking time to consider how well it suits you and your needs. You might find that while you do want to make some changes, these can be phased over time. Most changes involving structural features, such as patios and paths, can be done at any time when there isn't a hard frost that will prevent mortar and cement from setting, but changes involving plants are usually best carried out in spring and autumn.

However, you may not have inherited an established garden in good order. You may have bought a new house and even a new house sitting in a sea of builders' rubble and mud! Or you may have taken on a completely overgrown or unsuitable garden. In these cases, the planning stage is vital if you are to get a good return on your efforts.

- Ideally you should make a scale drawing of the plot, taking into account the factors mentioned in Chapter 02 such as soil, aspect, etc. If you like drawing you will enjoy this phase. If you don't, on a sheet of paper roughly draw the shape of the garden and mark where you want the principal features to go. At this stage, it is enough to write 'lawn', 'bed', 'patio', etc. When you mark it out on the actual site you will get a much better idea how it will look. For a precise style, such as a formal garden, your planning will need to be more detailed.
- Once you know what you want, mark it out in the garden using pegs and string, sand trickled through a funnel, or a garden hose. You will need to take account of the height of any features and how large your plants will grow.

For many people it is unlikely that the whole plan will be executed immediately, and there is no harm in creating your garden design bit by bit as long as you are still following an overall scheme that will eventually bring the whole garden together. In fact, putting your plans into practice in stages is often a good thing as it allows you to make alterations – what you have mapped out on paper does not always turn into the reality you expect. Whatever changes you make, it is important that the garden has a unified structure and is not simply a collection of disjointed elements. It will work best if you design it so that the different areas lead into one another – paths, arches, curved beds and even steps all provide good linking features.

You can alter the feel of your garden without making major structural changes. Using colour is a good way to achieve this. Hot colours, such as reds and oranges, will make flowers stand out and the garden seem lively, whereas strong blues will make it feel cooler and soft shades, such as mauves, pale blues and pinks, will make it soothing and restful.

This chapter gives you some basic ideas and advice on creating garden styles in your own space. If you try to copy an exact 'look', you will be restricting the range of features you can include. For example, in a strictly formal garden it will be hard to incorporate a lot of wild flowers or a children's play area. In reality, most people have a mixture of styles in their garden, however small, but they usually link up to make a unified picture. In any case, the most important thing is to have what you yourself want.

Here are some features you may need to take into account in your garden design:

- tool/bicycle/car storage
- patio
- barbecues and eating areas
- washing line
- rubbish areas (household and garden)
- compost bins
- bonfire site
- play area
- summer house/conservatory
- water features
- swimming pools
- paths
- areas for pets
- trellis/pergola
- anything to increase privacy and reduce noise
- containers
- trees
- kitchen garden
- area for cut flowers
- herb garden
- greenhouse.

Privacy and boundaries

Very few of us have as much space or privacy as we would like. Most people want their gardens to be somewhere private to relax with their friends and family, so this becomes extremely important in garden design. Total privacy, especially from sound, is hard to achieve, but it is generally possible to reach acceptable levels. Most people worry more about being overlooked (or overlooking things they don't like) than overheard; while only really unpleasant smells, such as choking smoke or rotting dustbins are of concern to us. Good, considerate relations with your immediate neighbours help, for instance, avoiding lighting a big bonfire with the wind blowing in their direction when they are having a party in their garden! The two main ways to obtain privacy are:

1 Choosing a suitable layout of the garden itself, which is mostly a matter of common sense. For example, if you don't want to be overlooked you need to find a space that both benefits from enough light and warmth and where there is no line of sight contact (after you've altered any boundary fences or hedges) with people that you might object seeing you.
2 Careful selection of the nature and size of boundary fences, hedges, etc.

These are the most important vertical elements in any garden and you need some sort of boundary between your land and that of your neighbour. If you do not like what is there, you can, within reason, alter it but remember that certain properties may have responsibility for their boundaries and you may also need permission from the relevant authorities for structural changes. It is common sense to try to agree changes to shared boundaries with your neighbours before you begin.

Boundaries can also block unattractive views, create privacy and security, help control animals or children, provide support for plants, offer protection from wind and sun and provide backdrops for the rest of the garden. Upright structures or plants are good for disguising things. Shrubs can fill in gaps and climbers, like roses, honeysuckle and clematis, can be grown over trellis or threaded through hedges. However, deciduous climbers will only obscure things from view while they are still in leaf.

Fences and walls

These are probably the most common types of boundary. Most fences are relatively cheap and easy to construct and do not take up too much room, while a bushy hedge can easily encroach a metre or so into your garden. Fence panels with trellis on top work well. The fence, if the posts reach the top of the trellis, gives solidity and the trellis offers privacy and support for climbers without losing too much light (once boundaries are above eye level more is lost in light than gained in privacy by going much higher). Since fences and walls last a long time, choose new ones carefully – their style and material should be both in keeping with the house and garden, and be strong enough – wooden uprights need treatment to prevent rot and to be buried in metal sleeves or concrete. Walls need good foundations, damp courses if they adjoin a house, and copings on top to prevent erosion by rain.

Strong winds will push over a completely solid fence so ideally about 40 per cent should be left open, letting wind through but slowing it down enough to prevent damage. More privacy can be offered by creepers.

Fences should be treated annually to prevent rot but, if this isn't possible (e.g. where climbers grow), at least check every spring and autumn that they are still in good repair and firmly fixed in the ground.

table 3.1 different types of fences and walls

Type	Description	Advantages	Disadvantages
Post and rail	Vertical posts with two or three horizontal rails attached	Cheap. Chain link can be added to provide a barrier and support for plants	No privacy. Does not stop wind or prevent access to property
Closeboard fencing	Posts with horizontal arris rails and vertical boards nailed to them	Strong, especially if made out of oak or deal. Suits most styles and works well with trellis	Expensive. Will not support climbers unless wire or trellis is added
Lapboard fencing	Machine woven slats made into panels	Cheap. Easy to put up	Not particularly attractive. Not as strong as closeboard
Picket fencing	Arris rails with flay poles nailed, usually at 5-cm/ 2-in intervals	Cheap and easy to put up. Especially suitable for cottage styles. Looks good painted	Does not provide privacy or a solid barrier. Will only support small climbers

Woven hurdles	Panels made of woody stems (hazels or osiers – willow shoots) woven between uprights	Easy to put up. Good wind channel. Matches plants well and good for climbers	Not very sturdy, unless well fixed to uprights.
Chestnut paling	Halved chestnut stakes held together with wire	Rolls up. Easy to install. Good temporary measure while waiting for a hedge to grow	Not very sturdy
Trellis	Thin batons fixed in square or diamond pattern. Some expands	Good for increasing the height of existing fences. Provides support for climbers	Can be flimsy. Make sure it is strong enough to support the climber when fully grown
Walls	Stone or brick	Long lasting, attractive. Can be used to link house and garden	Expensive. Must be well built with foundations, copings and damp course if joined to buildings
Iron	Metal posts with iron cross bars	Most suited for front gardens of town houses	Expensive. Does not provide privacy
Wire	Wire mesh fixed to vertical posts, usually concrete	Good support for climbers. Will keep animals in or out. Allows light and wind to pass through	Can look unattractive. Does not provide privacy. Usually best clothed in climbers

Hedges

Hedges take up more space than fences or walls but provide a very good barrier and block out noises, such as passing traffic. If you are planting from new, the main decisions are whether the hedges should be evergreen or deciduous, formal or informal. Hornbeam or beech leaves turn brown in autumn without falling, providing interesting winter colour. Informal hedges often take up more room than formally cut evergreens, although flowering shrubs like berberis can make attractive rather loose hedges.

Plants for a new hedge shouldn't be too big or planted too close together. Smaller plants (up to 45 cm/18 in) will settle in quicker and grow faster in the long run. For most hedging plants 90 cm/ 3 ft is about the right distance apart – they will do best planted in early winter so that their roots can become properly established before the top starts growing in spring.

Until established (at least three years), you will need to water your hedge and keep the base free of weeds. Afterwards, the only maintenance needed is pruning – trimming it at least once a year (possibly more if fast growing or you want a particular shape – see the 'Pruning' section in Chapter 07, page 127).

table 3.2 different types of hedging

Type	Deciduous (D) or evergreen (E)	Fast or slow growing	Comments
Berberis darwinii	E	Medium	Flowers in spring, berries in autumn
Berberis thunbergii	D	Medium	Many have interesting leaf colours in autumn
Buxus sempervirens (Box)	E	Slow	Good for low hedging
Carpinus betulus (Hornbeam)	D	Fairly fast	Leaves change colour but do not drop. Likes clay soil

Type	Deciduous (D) or evergreen (E)	Fast or slow growing	Comments
Chamaecyparis lawsoniana (Lawson cypress)	E	Fairly fast on most soils, slow on chalk	Be careful to choose the right size; cultivars range from dwarf to 35 m/ 115 ft!
Corylus avellana (Hazel)	D	Fairly fast	Best in large gardens. Can be pruned to control size. Catkins in early spring
x *Cupressocyparis leylandii* (Leyland cypress)	E	Very, very fast	Needs a minimum height and spread of 2.5 m/ 8ft and can reach 23 m/ 80 ft. Unpopular with neighbours!
Fagus sylvatica (Beech)	D	Fairly fast	Chalky soil. Leaves turn brown but do not drop. Good windbreak
Ilex aquifolium (Holly)	E	Slow, but tolerates any soil	Variegated leaves and berries can provide interest. Plant male and female plants
Lavandula (Lavender)	E	Low growing only	Needs full sun. Do not prune into old wood
Ligustrum (Privet)	E	Fast, any soil	Prune twice a year

Lonicera nitida (Chinese honeysuckle)	E	Fast	Small flowers followed by berries
Prunus	E	Fast or fairly fast	*P. laurocerasus* (Cherry laurel) or *P. lusitanica* (Portugal laurel). Both large
Pyracantha (Firethorn)	E	Fast	Berries in winter. Spiny stems. Suitable for exposed site
Quercus ilex (Holm oak)	E	Slow	Large imposing hedge. Good windbreak
Taxus baccata (Yew)	E	Very slow	Good dense hedge, can be kept narrow
Thuja plicata (Western red cedar)	E	Fast. Tolerant of shade and chalk	Conifer. Dark green, gold and blue-green varieties available

Table 3.2 is only a small selection of possible hedging plants: *Cotoneaster*, *Crataegus* (Hawthorn), *Elaeagnus, Escallonia, Euonymus japonicus*, *Osmanthus* x *burkwoodii, Rosmarinus officinalis* (Rosemary), *Rosa* (especially *R. rugosa*) and *Spirea* are all suitable for informal hedges.

Family gardens

Family gardens are probably the most common type of garden and the least fixed in style since they need to adapt constantly to the changing needs of family members. A family garden design should allow individual features or areas to be changed without disrupting the overall pattern. For example, an outgrown sandpit can easily be converted into a pond. With young children, safety is the major priority. Ponds or water features should be fenced off and poisonous plants avoided. Children are another good reason to garden organically, avoiding sprays and slug pellets.

The play area for young children needs to be near the house or seating area so you can keep an eye on them; for older children the play area is better hidden away further down the garden for your benefit and theirs! Swings, climbing frames and rough grass for ball games can be positioned behind a hedge if you have room.

You need to list all your requirements for a family garden and then see which ones are compatible. Realistically, when they're young your family is more important than your garden. You may want fine display flowerbeds but it is better to start with tough low maintenance shrubs and gradually change to more delicate flowers once football is no longer a threat. Always make the patio area larger rather than smaller: it can act as a play area when the grass is wet and if you are eating outdoors you can never have too much space. Position your ornaments and containers carefully. Be sure to provide enough seating and, equally importantly, storage space. Bicycles, toys, paddling pools and soft chairs all need to be stored somewhere, ideally separately from the tool shed.

Children will view the garden as a play area, although they can enjoy helping you with simple garden tasks like raking up leaves and digging. If you give children their own patch to look after, make sure you choose a sunny spot with well-nourished soil.

When time is tight

Many people have limited time for their gardens. Plan carefully; choose the right plants, and then your garden that will require very little maintenance after the first couple of years. Plants that can look after themselves are essential: if planted closely weeds will find it much harder to grow between them.

- It may be worth replacing your lawn with paving or gravel. You can still get the effect of greenery from low maintenance evergreen shrubs or grasses. If you keep it, let the grass grow a little longer and plant some wild flowers to give the feel of a meadow.
- If you prefer shorter grass, tougher grass types, for example, mixtures based on perennial rye grass, will need cutting less

often. Features like island beds, sharp corners to the lawn and overhanging trees are all time consuming to mow around.
- In a children's play area you could substitute grass with bark as a surface.

Other tips include:

- Divide your garden into a series of rooms using hedges, trellis and climbers and then only garden intensively in one or two.
- Natural ponds require more maintenance than artificial pools or fountains.
- Mulch bare soil to prevent weeds.
- Avoid bedding plants because they need to be changed twice yearly, but scatter seed, such as nasturtiums and poppies, randomly in the garden and some of it will germinate quite quickly. Choose perennials like peonies that will look after themselves if put in the right soil and place.
- Make sure you choose the right plants for your soil, water and light levels and position – they'll take far less effort.
- Grasses can look interesting, especially in paved areas or gravel, and may only need to be cut back in spring.

Water is a scarce resource and if metered an expensive one.

- Avoid sprays and sprinklers and use trickle irrigation systems.
- Raised beds (but set on soil to ensure good drainage) offer alternatives to containers.
- Locate taps in the right position for hoses.
- As hosepipe bans become more frequent, water butts, raised up high enough to allow a can underneath a tap at the base, will save you a lot of effort.

When planting your garden, consider how to give it some style as well as keeping it simple to look after. Choose the vertical elements carefully since they make such a strong impact on your garden but can vary hugely in cost and maintenance requirements.

Walls virtually look after themselves but they are expensive to build; fences and trellis need to be treated with preservative, but bamboo screens last without any treatment. Pierced concrete block is cheap, maintenance-free and its outlines can be softened with climbers. Hedges can be an easy option if you choose plants that don't need too much trimming.

You need to think about flat surfaces too, because they are difficult to alter once they are in place. Paving slabs with well-mortared joints are probably the most straightforward option, although brick and concrete are easy to look after. Decking must be well preserved and needs regular treatment. Gravel can be used instead of paving, even on quite large areas. Firstly, lay a geo-textile membrane down to stop weeds growing through. For ease of walking, the depth of gravel should not exceed 2.5 cm/1 in and the pebble size is best kept to between 5–12 mm/2–5 in approximately.

Some brief notes on a few popular gardening styles follow, but the best way to decide what you like is to visit good gardens – see 'Taking it further' on page 194.

Cottage gardens

These gardens look back nostalgically to the image of a country cottage surrounded by flowers, although the originals were hard work to maintain. They need time to develop for best effect and planting has to make the best use of space, combining all sorts of flowers and often vegetables. Such gardens look particularly attractive at the front of houses where you can have a path leading up to the front door, surrounded by a riot of colour on both sides, with its edges softened by plants spilling over from the adjoining beds. Wooden fences and locally sourced materials work best if you decide to keep a patio next to the house.

Formal gardens

Formal gardens are in many respects the opposite of cottage gardens. They use a limited range of plants, each precisely placed and have a high proportion of hard landscaping, a strong emphasis on symmetry and simple geometrical shapes, and a rigid overall plan. Traditionally associated with large, expensive palaces, the style is actually very adaptable and you can take elements of formal gardens and use them successfully on even the smallest plot. The design can be based on geometric shapes with clear changes of height and direction, using clipped evergreens as 'punctuation', and water, contained in hard-edged formal shapes, to provide reflection and possibly movement and sound.

Jungle and tropical gardens

One of the best reasons for making a garden is to feel, on entering it, that you are transported somewhere entirely different, away from all the bustle of work and the world outside. Exotic and jungle gardens achieve this with an overload to the senses and imagination. Until recently, such collections of plants tended to be kept in public gardens or expensive conservatories since they were expensive to buy and generally could not survive a cold English winter. However, changing climate conditions and a greater supply of cheaper suitable plants now make them far more suitable for ordinary gardens, although the plants are different from ordinary ones with large spectacular leaves or flowers.

Meadow gardens

One of the big trends of recent times has been a move away from formal borders to a more meadow-like approach with plants positioned naturalistically and used for their sculptural qualities. They are dealt with in more detail in Chapter 05 ('Lawns and meadows', page 76) but the idea of a meadow garden is simple – you need to create a piece of land that offers approximately the variety and profusion of wild flowers that would have been more commonplace in, say, the nineteenth century.

International gardens

In this age of globalization, garden designs and philosophies from all over the world have become established, often successfully, in other countries. Oriental (and especially Japanese) gardens transfer particularly well to almost all climates, at least in part because of the limited plant content. They are full of symbolism, much of which is inevitably lost or misunderstood when the concept is exported. The famous remark of a Japanese Ambassador when asked to open a very expensive 'Japanese' garden in England was: 'This is really very interesting indeed – we have nothing at all like it in Japan!' The basic style is easy to recreate, however, achieving the main elements of simplicity, calm and order. Islamic gardens, often with central water features, have been copied throughout the world for over a thousand years and are particularly suited to courtyards, usually being designed around geometric patterns.

If temperatures continue to rise as expected, this sort of cool and peaceful garden is likely to become very popular. Likewise, Mediterranean gardening is more a climatic than a regional style, with features dictated by hot summers, low rainfall and mild winters. The bright blues, yellows, pinks and oranges used in Mediterranean regions look very good against brilliant sunshine.

Twentieth and twenty-first century designs

Throughout the twentieth century, gardening styles changed and many designers placed an increasing emphasis on hard landscaping and moved towards more minimalist planting schemes. Although plants remained important, they were now used in a different way. Rather than beds or borders filled with a multitude of plants, one or two specimen plants were used to create maximum impact. The use of hard landscaping, especially metal and glass, is one of the key aspects of a modern garden and you can get excellent ideas for them at the large flower shows.

Water gardens

Water looks good in any garden, offering the potential for reflection, sound and movement as well as a habitat for wildlife. Features come in such a great range of variety that it is easy to find a suitable one. They all need sound construction and many features will also need electricity. The construction of water features is beyond the scope of this book and many are better installed by professionals. Any electrical work *must* be carried out by a professional – water and electricity are potentially deadly if not handled correctly. The most important considerations when planning a water feature are that:

- it should fit in with the rest of your garden (even in winter)
- it doesn't need too much maintenance
- it should be safe – especially if you have children.

Wildlife gardens

A real wildlife garden requires considerably more planning and maintenance than you might expect – just leaving it alone is not enough. Because many plants ideally suited to attracting wildlife tend to be rampant or self-seed freely, they can take over a large area. Therefore, it is easier to create a good environment for wildlife in a big garden, although you can still succeed on a city patio. Without imitating the wild it is enough to choose the right plants and create the right environments. Dense planting offers hiding places for animals, and if you want wildlife you must not use any chemical herbicides or insecticides. Feed the garden as naturally as possible – making your own compost heap will help you to do this and will also act as a valuable habitat for small animals. Attracting insects at the bottom of the food chain makes the rest automatically follow. Putting out food and growing trees and shrubs with edible berries will also attract a range of birds, mammals and insects. See the lists below for some good choices of plants.

Plants to attract birds

Berberis thunbergii, *Cotoneaster*, *Crataegus* (Hawthorn), *Daphne*, *Hedera* (Ivy), *Malus sylvestris* (Crab apple), *Papaver somniferum* (Opium poppy), *Prunus padus* (Bird cherry), *Pyracantha* (Firethorn), *Sambucus nigra* (Elder), *Sorbus aucuparia* (Rowan), *Viburnum*

Plants to attract insects and butterflies

Aster (Michaelmas daisy), *Aubretia*, *Buddleja davidii*, *Centaurea* (Cornflower), *Dianthus* (Pinks), *Escallonia*, *Hebe* (Veronica), *Hyssopus officinalis*, *Lavandula* (Lavender), *Lonicera* (Honeysuckle), *Mentha suaveolens* (Apple mint), *Myosotis* (Forget-me-not), *Nicotiana* (Tobacco plant), *Oreganum vulgare* (Marjoram), *Papaver orientale* (Oriental poppy), *Phlox*, *Sedum*, *Syringa* (Lilac), *Tagetes* (Marigold), *Thymus* (Thyme), *Viola* (Pansy)

Seasons

More thought and planning are needed to keep your garden looking good throughout the year, especially in the cold dark months of winter, than in summer alone. From late spring until early autumn, most plants will look at their best. If you want a winter garden, you need to concentrate on the parts of the garden visible from the house in winter or plant only one or two areas of a larger garden to provide winter colour – as long as you position them well the eye will be drawn to these areas and away from the dormant rest of the garden. Plants with coloured stems, berries, variegated foliage or scent are particularly useful and look good against a background of evergreens, but remember evergreens are more vulnerable to snow than deciduous plants – shake them off after a heavy fall.

Cutting gardens

Older, larger gardens, especially Edwardian ones, often had a separate portion to provide cut flowers for the house. A splendid example has been restored in the walled gardens at West Dean in Sussex, England. This style of garden has recently undergone a revival of interest, but it is labour intensive and needs space. An easier way is to grow flowers for cutting among others in a normal garden or combined with vegetables.

If you choose the correct varieties they will produce more flowers to replace the ones you cut. A few of the most suitable are listed below:

Flowers for cutting

Amaranthus caudatus (Love lies bleeding), *Ammi majus* (Bishop's flower), *Anemone, Antirrhinum* (Snapdragon), *Calendula* (Marigold), *Centaurea* (Cornflower), *Centranthus ruber* (Red valerian), *Cleome* (Spider flower), *Cosmos*, *Dahlia*, *Helianthus annus* (Sunflower), *Lathyrus odoratus* (Sweet pea), *Lunaria* (Honesty), *Matthiola* (Stock), *Mollucella laevis* (Bells of Ireland), *Nicotiana sylvestris* (Tobacco plant), *Nigella damascena* (Love-in-a-mist), *Phlox*, *Scabiosa* (Pincushion flower), *Verbena bonariensis*, *Zinnia*

04 courtyards and patios

In this chapter you will learn:

- **how to create a perfect patio**
- **tricks to make gardens look bigger**
- **different options for patios and paths**
- **about buying furniture and equipment.**

Introduction

A patio may form part of a larger garden or take up the whole area of a small one as a courtyard. Building a patio as part of an existing garden is a big task so it is important you get it right first time.

- Position the patio correctly. The most practical place may seem near the house, but consider other options – it may be nice to walk down a path and either sit in a totally secluded area or look back at the house. Either way, it needs to be easily accessible and well lit if you are considering sitting out in the evening. Take into account when you will most use the patio and whether you want it to be in the sun or the shade.
- Make the patio as large as possible. You need to be able to fit a table and chairs on it and still allow room to walk around. If you find it is too large, you can always fill it up with some big containers.
- If the patio joins directly to the lawn, make the level slightly lower than the grass as this will make mowing much easier. The level should be higher than surrounding flowerbeds to prevent earth overflowing.
- The edges of the patio can be softened or modified by planting.
- If you want to change the position of an existing patio, wait a few months – the previous owners may have had a logical reason for siting it where they did, such as getting the evening sun, etc.

Courtyards need to be carefully designed because on a small scale every detail is important. In large gardens it is often possible to disguise unattractive features, such as an old shed, while in a small garden any fault will tend to stand out. There are advantages to gardening on a small scale though, and as enclosed courtyards can be very sheltered you may find that you can grow a greater range of plants than on a more exposed site in the same area. Small gardens can be given a greater sense of space by using a few tricks:

- Plant the beds with a mixture of tall and short plants.
- For privacy, trellis with climbers does not take up as much room as a hedge and does not block out as much light as a tall fence or wall. A good combination is to have a fence or wall up to 1.6–1.8 m/5–6 ft and then trellis on top.
- An arbour will provide privacy and a certain amount of shade depending on how thickly you train the plants over it.

- Lighting can be used to create illusions of greater space.
- Formal water features usually work better in small spaces, and the sound of flowing water can enhance the peace of a city courtyard.
- If you want to plant a tree, bear in mind what its roots may do to surrounding buildings and where it will cast shadows. Any of the trees listed in Chapter 05 (see page 59) would be suitable.
- Trellis, mirrors or even *trompe-l'oeil* can create the illusion of a greater area of garden, but these features must be positioned carefully to be effective. Always try to position mirrors so that they reflect part of the garden rather than the people in it. You want to create the impression of more space, rather than more people!

Materials

In any patio or courtyard, regardless of size, the most important element in terms of basic design is the material from which it is made. Plants can be moved or altered, but the feel of the area will be largely determined by what material you use as its base since this will form the backdrop for everything else. The main materials available for this use are listed below, together with their pros and cons:

Natural stone

This group includes stones such as York stone and sandstone. Most look very good, particularly if they echo the stone of surrounding buildings. The downsides are that they tend to be expensive, heavy and can be slippery when wet.

Paving slabs

A huge variety is available, ranging from good imitations of natural stone to cheap slabs. They also come in a great variety of shapes including hexagonal, octagonal and circular. If creating a pattern, be careful to what extent it stands out – the use of greatly contrasting colours can be dominating. Take care when buying pre-cast slabs; although they are often cheap, they can also be brittle and break easily.

Concrete

This is versatile and can be used to infill most spaces, but it can look dull and is usually better if used in conjunction with another material such as brick edging.

Bricks

These can look lovely but are dark and therefore not always suitable for a small shady garden. They can be laid in interesting patterns, such as herringbone, and set to fit most shaped areas. If you are planning an area, make sure you have enough similar bricks as different types will stand out unattractively.

Slate

This can look interesting, but tends to be dark and dominating. It can also be very slippery when wet.

Decking

Hardwood decking is versatile and combines particularly well with gravel, plants and water. The wood must be well treated and can be prone to slipperiness and rot. To a certain extent, the danger of slipping can be reduced by covering the area with fine chicken-wire nailed down at regular intervals. A great variety of natural colours and patterns is available. Use these to create interest as a large area of identical planks all going the same way can look monotonous.

Gravel, pebbles and granite sets

All these surfaces tend to be too uneven for patios if you intend to use the area for sitting. They are more suited to paths and areas that do not need to be completely level.

Paths

Any garden that is larger than a courtyard will need paths of some sort. Apart from being practical, paths can add interest to the garden. A curved path can be used to make a small garden look larger by giving the impression that it winds away to another area that is out of sight. Even if you do not have such an area, you can always create a focal point towards which your path can lead such as a statue, a fountain or an urn of flowers.

Any of the materials in the section above are suitable for paths. Before laying a path, think carefully about who will use it – small children and wheelchair users will need wide level paths, as will people carrying food to a patio or barbecue. On the other hand, a path to encourage interest or protect the lawn in winter can simply consist of stepping stones. When laying stepping stones, make sure it is easy to step from one to the next, otherwise people will simply ignore them and trample on the lawn or plants in between. As with patios, paths are best laid below the level of the grass but above that of flowerbeds.

Furniture and equipment

Your furniture needs to be sturdy enough to remain out all year unless you have space to store it during wet weather and winter. Wood, plastic or metals are the most hardwearing options. Bright colours or white will stand out whereas green or black will blend with the surroundings.

Lighting needs to be planned right at the start unless you are going to rely solely on candles. You do not want your garden lit too brightly but you do need to be able to see where you are walking and what you are eating.

Barbecues do not help the environment but they do bring great pleasure. They range from simple disposable trays to elaborate fixed systems. If you want one, take into account how often you will use it and buy accordingly.

Patio heaters are another matter and do a proportionally great amount of harm by churning out heat, much of which is lost as it floats up into the air. Consider how much you would really benefit from having one – do you really want to sit out in the garden when it is that cold?

plants

In this chapter you will learn:

- **types of plants and how to make the most of them**
- **how to choose the best plants for your needs**
- **about masses of different climbers**
- **all about lawns, meadows and the alternatives you could have.**

Introduction

Plants are likely to be the main feature of your garden so it is worth understanding a little about them. They will be changing all the time as they grow, both seasonally and in terms of size. It will be obvious if plants are not well or happy so it is really worth choosing the right plant for the right place. All plants are roughly the same; they have roots, stems, leaves and flowers or seeds of some kind.

- The large roots anchor the plant and transport water and nutrients up into the plant. The small hair-like roots take the water and nutrients from the soil. Some roots also store energy for the plant. Many roots are much nearer the surface than you would imagine.
- Stems carry the water and nutrients up into the plant. They may be almost non-existent as in the case of a low bulb or huge as in the case of a tall tree.
- Leaves convert energy from the sun, carbon from the air and water into food for the plant. They lose water as it evaporates from pores on their undersides and more is then drawn up through the plant.
- Flowers are the means by which most plants reproduce. Their colour, shape and fragrance are all designed to aid pollination. Some plants spread by putting out new roots but most need to produce fertile seeds to carry on the next generation.
- All plants need light, water, air, nutrients and good soil, albeit to varying degrees.
- Plants differ in their ability to deal with cold, and their optimum conditions are either described in terms of hardiness or zones. Hardiness describes how tough the plant is and zones describe the areas where the plant will grow. Neither are dependent solely on temperature but are also influenced by humidity, distance from the sea, prevailing wind and temperature fluctuations. These are not firm divisions because much depends on local conditions but they are a useful guideline.

When choosing plants you need to take several things into account:

- The plants you want must be able to grow in your garden.
- Consider size, colour and shape.

- Check how fast the plant will grow and how long it will last; annuals give instant results but only last a matter of months while trees may continue growing for several centuries.
- Consider how your plants will fit together in the garden. As a general rule, taller plants should be at the back or centre of a bed with the smallest specimens at the front. A degree of variation will add interest, as will the use of see-through plants, such as *Verbena bonariensis* and *Thalictrum delavayi*, which will give height but will not create a solid barrier.
- The accepted rule is that you should arrange plants in groups of odd numbers, that is, a clump of three, as this looks more natural. If you have the space, this is a good rule to follow. If your garden is small, you will not have room for this approach so be careful when using single plants that the overall effect is not bitty with different plants all fighting for attention.
- Consider the timings of your plants. It is no use having two stunning plants each vying for your attention at exactly the same time and then dying back together. Equally, a lot of emphasis is often placed on the importance of winter interest in a garden and yes, you do need plants which look good at that time of year but probably not more than a couple.

Trees

A tree will give height, shade and a feeling of maturity to any garden regardless of its size. Trees also produce large amounts of oxygen, filter out pollutants from the air, and provide homes for animals and insects. They hold the soil in place and enrich it with their fallen leaves.

Trees may not seem as varied as shrubs but there are still several things you need to consider before planting one:

- evergreen or deciduous
- flowering or non-flowering
- scent
- autumn colour
- interesting bark
- fruit
- check its final size – when studying plant lists check the sizes given are those at maturity and not just after ten years; most trees reach their full size at twenty years but some will go on increasing in size for a hundred years!

Trees should not be planted too near buildings (as a rough guide, the roots will spread out as far as the final spread of the branches), and you should take into account the shade they will create. Furthermore, depending on the tree, plants may not grow beneath it. When choosing a tree try to ensure it has at least two seasons of interest, for example, blossom, autumn colour, fruits or good winter shape. If you have a large garden you will have a vast range of trees to choose from. If you have a small garden you will need to be more careful, and below is a selection of attractive trees suitable for restricted spaces.

Trees for small spaces

Most of the trees listed below will not grow much beyond 10 m/ 30 ft tall and 8 m/25 ft wide. The ones described as 'tiny' will remain under 2 m/6 ft. This is a small selection of trees that all give you a lot for your space, looking good for the greater part of the year. Many can be further restricted by growing in a container but they will need extra care (see Chapter 08).

Acer japonicum, A. palmatum (Japanese maple) – Japanese maples have beautifully shaped palmate leaves that turn fantastic colours in autumn. Many varieties can be kept tiny if grown in a container.

Amelanchier canadensis – white flowers in spring, small blue-black fruits in summer and fine orange and red leaves in autumn. Drought tolerant.

Arbutus unedo (Strawberry tree) – evergreen with attractive, rough, reddish-brown bark and small white or pinkish flowers in autumn that ripen to red and orange fruits the following year.

Cercis – heart-shaped leaves and clusters of bright pink or red flowers in spring. *C. canadensis* 'Forest Pansy' has reddish-purple leaves and *C. siliquastrum* (Judas tree) has blue-green leaves that turn yellow in autumn.

Citrus – *C. limon* (Lemon) and *C. sinensis* (Orange) will both make tiny trees if grown in containers. Both need protection from cold to fruit well.

Cornus kuosa var. *chinensis* (Dogwood) – ornamental, flaking bark, dark green leaves that turn crimson in autumn and creamy-white flowers which fade to pink.

Crataegus (Hawthorn) – white or deep pink flowers, small round fruits and good autumn colour. Hawthorns are extremely tough and look attractive almost all year round. *C. laevigata* 'Paul's Scarlet' has wonderful, double, dark pink flowers.

Fruit trees – can be kept compact if grown on dwarf rootstock.

Lagerstromeria indica (Crepe flower) – interesting peeling bark and crinkly flowers in white, pink, red or purple throughout summer. Protect from frost by growing against a warm wall.

Laurus nobilis (Bay) – slow-growing tree which can be kept tiny in a container. The evergreen leaves are useful in cooking and there are yellow flowers in spring followed by small black berries.

Malus (Crab apple) – most remain reasonably small. Many varieties combine fragrant pink or white blossom in spring, edible fruits and good autumn colour.

Olea europaea (Olive) – attractively shaped evergreen tree with white flowers in summer followed by edible fruits that turn from green to black as they ripen. Will remain tiny in a container but needs a mild, Mediterranean climate to survive and fruit well.

Prunus (Ornamental cherry) – most ornamental cherries remain reasonably compact and all have fabulous pink or white blossom in autumn or spring, depending on the variety. *P.* 'Amanogawa' (flagpole cherry), *P.* 'Kanzan', *P. mume* and *P.* x *subhirtella* are all good choices.

Salix caprea 'Kilmarnock' (Kilmarnock willow) – a tiny willow. The branches form an umbrella shape and have fluffy silver catkins in mid- to late spring.

Shrubs including roses

In the gardening scheme of things shrubs come between trees and perennials. They usually have several woody stems, can be deciduous or evergreen and range in size from low ground-cover plants to large bushes. The dividing line between large shrubs and small trees is vague. Lilac is a typical example that can appear within either classification. Most climbers, roses, soft fruit bushes and even many herbs also fall within the shrub category.

You can create entire beds with shrubs, mix them with perennials, annuals and bulbs or use them singly as specimen plants. The main uses for shrubs are as follows:

- Permanent colour to act as a backdrop or hide an eyesore. Evergreens are usually best as they will provide a constant layer. You can always get seasonal interest with climbers or shorter plants in front.
- Specimen plants that will look spectacular at a particular time. Balance these shrubs so they work in succession; there is no point if everything looks its best at the same time.
- Plants to fill a large awkward area such as a very dark corner.
- Plants that will act as protection for smaller or more delicate specimens.
- Fragrance (see the list below).

Shrubs usually take two to three years to become established and many need little or no maintenance. Pruning is normally the only task and this is not nearly as complicated as it might seem; it is covered in detail in Chapter 07. As with trees, always check the final size of any shrub.

Fragrant shrubs

Buddleja – many buddleja are fragrant, especially *B. auriculata* which is an evergreen bush with small creamy-white, pink- or orange-centred flowers in autumn.

Daphne – *D. bholua* and *D.* x *burkwoodii* cultivars have particularly fragrant flowers in late winter and late spring respectively.

Hamamelis (Witch hazel) – deciduous bush with fragrant, spidery-like flowers in autumn and winter. The flowers may be yellow, orange or dark red.

Philadelphus (Mock orange) – deciduous bush with white flowers in summer. The cup-shaped flowers can be single or double and may be tinged with pink.

Rosa (Rose) – many roses have highly fragrant flowers, especially the old varieties and most English roses.

Sarcococca (Christmas box) – evergreen bush with small, fragrant, white flowers in winter.

Syringa (Lilac) – deciduous bush or tree with conical flowers in late spring. The flowers may be white, pink, purple or crimson.

Viburnum – deciduous or evergreen bush. Most have clusters of tiny pink or white flowers in winter or early spring, *V.* x *bodnantense* and *V.* x *burkwoodii* are especially fragrant.

Roses

Roses are particularly important shrubs because of their amazing flowers and their range and versatility. At first the choice may seem overwhelming, but roses can be divided into fairly distinctive groups and, unless you are going to specialize, there is a reasonably small selection to suit most tastes and requirements.

- Species roses are wild roses and can easily be recognized in catalogues as they only have Latin names. They have not been interbred and are the ancestors of most ramblers. Many can be rampant, they flower once with small highly scented flowers, and later develop attractive hips.
- Old roses tend to be highly regarded in the rose world. They have romantic names and many date back to Ancient Greece and Rome. They are mostly fairly large shrubs (1.5–2 m/5–7 ft) and usually flower once in midsummer. Flower shapes, colour, toughness, fragrance and a short but spectacular display are the reasons for choosing these roses. The main shrub groups are Alba, Bourbon, Centifolia, China, Damask, Gallica, Moss and Sweet Briar. Boursault, Noisette and Tea are climbers.
- Modern roses include large-flowered or hybrid tea, cluster-flowered or floribunda, many miniatures and shrubs. Most were developed in the twentieth century and are often looked down on as many lost the charm and fragrance of old roses in order to achieve reliable repeat flowering.
- English roses have been developed from the 1970s onwards by David Austin in England, and new varieties are being added all the time. The best ones have the scent and flower shape of old roses but repeat reliably, are tough and come in a greater range of colours. In most cases these are the roses to choose.
- Climbing roses cross all the earlier classifications. They have fairly stiff stems and large flowers, some of which are scented and most of which repeat well.
- Rambler roses have more flexible stems than climbers and bear a large number of little flowers in clusters in midsummer. The display only lasts a few weeks but can be amazing. Ramblers do best where they can drape over something such as a tree or building. Although they do not repeat, the flowers are usually very fragrant. Be careful to choose the right size, some such as 'Wedding Day' are very large and can reach 9 m/30 ft.

All roses have good points but few can combine everything so you need to choose which features are important to you.

- Size – roses range from low ground-cover plants and tiny patio specimens to climbers which will cover a house.
- Flowering – some roses flower once in midsummer; others flower in midsummer and again in autumn; and a third group flower continuously from midsummer right through until autumn or even winter as long as they are regularly deadheaded.
- Scent – not all roses are scented; if you want a long flowering period you may lose fragrance.
- Hips – some roses have amazing hips which give added interest through the winter.
- Flower shape – single flowers have eight or less petals, are usually fairly flat and delicate looking. Doubles can have up to 40 petals and are much rounder. There is a wide range of semi-doubles in between in varying shapes.

Bear in mind the following when planting roses.

- Most roses need to be sheltered from strong winds.
- Most roses prefer neutral or acid clay soil. If you have light soil, enrich it well first with organic matter.
- You should not plant a rose on the site where another one has been recently growing. This is because it is likely to get 'rose sickness' or 'specific rose transplant disease' which can remain in the soil for several years after the removal of a previous rose. If you cannot avoid planting in the same place, you need to remove the surrounding soil to a depth of 25 cm/ 10 in and replace it. You can use the soil elsewhere in the garden.
- Roses are greedy plants and benefit from a good mulch of well-rotted farmyard manure in spring. If you are mixing roses with other plants, such as annuals or perennials, leave room for this mulch as many smaller plants will not appreciate it.

Perennials including grasses

The strict definition of a perennial is a plant that lives for more than three seasons, but in gardening terms it usually applies to non-woody plants that live two or more years. Many tender or short-lived perennials are often grown as annuals or biennials, for example, foxgloves, hollyhocks and snapdragons.

Many perennials are herbaceous, which means they die down to ground level in winter and re-grow from the base each spring. The disadvantage of this for the gardener is that they can look boring for a considerable part of the year. Some plants, such as poppies, have interesting seed heads but more die down or just collapse and look sad. The way round this seasonal drabness is to plant a mixed border that also includes shrubs, bulbs and annuals to fill in any gaps. It is worth bearing the following points in mind when choosing perennials.

- The requirements of the plant itself.
- Time and length of flowering season.
- Size and shape of the plant and the flowers.
- Fragrance – see the list on page 65.
- The size, shape and colour of the surrounding plants.

Perennials are easy to grow and give good results over a long period in return for your efforts. Most are best planted in mid-spring with a layer of mulch to conserve water. Tall perennials will need staking and many will flower repeatedly if deadheaded. Do not be tempted to feed and water them too much when they are young. Left within reason to their own devices they will grow into stronger plants.

Many perennials that flower in late summer or autumn benefit from the 'Chelsea Chop' in May. This is named after the Chelsea Flower Show that takes place in London at the same time. Cut back by a third or even more to create a more compact plant that will bear more flowers. The exact timing obviously depends on the weather but as a rough guide the plants should have reached about two-thirds of their final size. Make sure the plants are strong and healthy, cut back to a bud, and water and mulch afterwards. Echinacea, rudbeckia, helenium, bergamot (*Monarda*), sunflowers (*Helianthus*), phlox, Michaelmas daisies (*Aster*) and heliopsis all benefit from this treatment. In the late autumn, many need to be cut back to just above ground level and tender species should have their crowns covered with a light layer of dry leaves, straw or bark to protect them from frost. In spring, new growth will appear and any dead parts should be cut away. Every three or four years many perennials benefit from being dug up and divided. This is described under 'Propagation' in Chapter 07. Many perennials flower in the first year they are planted, provide a good display for several months and financially work out as better value than bought annuals because they do not have to be replaced each year.

Fragrant perennials

Cosmos astrosanguineus (Chocolate cosmos) – clump-forming plant with pale green leaves, red stems and velvety-maroon, chocolate-scented flowers in summer.

Hesperis matronalis (Sweet rocket) – short-lived perennial with hairy leaves and panicles of purple or white flowers throughout summer.

Monarda (Bergamot) – tall plant with big shaggy flowers from midsummer to early autumn and aromatic greeny-grey leaves.

Nicotiana sylvestris (Tobacco plant) – tall short-lived perennial with clusters of fine, tubular, white flowers in summer. The flowers close if exposed to bright sunlight.

Phlox paniculata – clumps of lance-shaped leaves and dome-shaped clusters of sweetly-scented flowers in summer and autumn. The flowers are red, blue, purple or white, often with contrasting centres.

Grasses

The term 'grasses' usually includes sedges, rushes and cats'-tails or bulrushes, which are not true grasses but do all look reasonably similar. All can be grown as individual specimens or in a bed along with other perennials, shrubs and annuals. Most are easy to grow but need an airy site to show them off to their best. Sedges need rich damp soil and like some shade, but grasses prefer poor soil and sunlight. If your soil is very rich it is best to dig in some grit or sand before planting. Grasses will survive in light shade but they stand more upright in sunlight. Many are drought tolerant and, once established, will need little watering. Although covered here, grasses are actually a mixture of annuals and perennials. Many spread by seed and you need to be careful that some of the more vigorous annuals do not turn into weeds. *Briza maxima* (greater quaking grass), and *Hordeum jubatum* (foxtail barley or squirrel tail grass) can both take over and so their flowers need to be deadheaded before they set seed.

Grasses may not have brightly coloured flowers, but they do have many other attractive features:

- The foliage can vary in colour from browns and greens through to the bright reds of Japanese blood grass (*Imperator cylindrical* 'Rubra').

- The leaves may be fine and delicate or flat and stiff and can range in size from 15 cm/6 in to over 4 m/12 ft.
- Many of the perennials, such as *Miscanthus sinensis* (eulalia grass), *Molinia caerulea* (moor grass) and *Panicum virgatum* (switch grass), have attractive seed heads which can be left over winter and cut back in spring.
- The flowers on grasses are usually small but often abundant and can form an impressive display. Miscanthus, panicum and pennisetum all have fine plumes or flowers throughout summer.
- Many grasses change colour with the seasons, for example, *Phalaris arundinacae* var. *picta* 'Feesy' has green and white leaves that are pinky in spring.
- Some grasses are evergreen, others look good as they fade. Many look amazing in the lower light levels of autumn and winter.
- Most grasses do not produce pollen but they are an important wildlife habitat.

Bamboos are woody grasses and can range in size from 30 cm to 20 m/12 in to 70 ft. Bearing this in mind, make sure you choose one that is the correct size for your garden. To a certain extent you can control their spread by mowing around them or restricting their roots by growing them in a container or by blocking the roots' path underground with a barrier such as polythene, sheet metal or concrete. Most bamboos like well-drained soil and should only need watering for the first couple of years while they get established.

Bulbs

This group includes corms, tubers and rhizomes that grow in a similar way to bulbs. There are also bulbous perennials that behave like a mixture of the two. Bulbs are made up of tightly packed fleshy leaves and mostly look like onions, for example, daffodils, tulips and lilies. Corms re-grow from the base of their stem each year and include crocuses and gladioli. Tubers are roots that have swollen so that they can store the necessary nutrients for the flower, for example, orchids and cyclamen. The final category, rhizomes, are actually swollen underground stems that store nutrients and spread out horizontally, for example, irises. In practice you rarely need to worry about the distinctions but they can be useful if you are looking for a particular plant in a catalogue or book.

All plants in this group store the nutrition they need within themselves. This is taken from sunlight through the leaves after flowering so it is very important that you do not cut the foliage back too soon when the flowers are over. Since the leaves have to be left to wither naturally, it is often better to grow bulbs through something, either grass, low-growing perennials or under shrubs whose growth will hide the fading leaves.

Most bulbs need good drainage and a certain amount of sunshine – cyclamen are about the only ones that will do well in the deep shade under evergreens. The lists below show some useful bulbs.

Winter to spring bulbs

Chionodoxa (Glory of the snow) – small, star-shaped, pink and blue flowers in early spring.

Crocus – thin grassy leaves and flowers in spring or autumn. The small goblet-shaped flowers are usually purple or yellow.

Galanthus (Snowdrop) – fine green or bluey-green leaves and pendant white flowers in late winter. The little flowers can have pale green markings.

Hyacinthoides non scripta (English bluebell) – the English bluebell is more dainty than its Spanish cousin (*H. hyspanica*) with small, scented, dangly blue flowers in spring. Shade tolerant.

Iris – a vast and confusing genus including some bulbs, ranging from tiny winter flowers to fans of sword-shaped leaves with tall blooms. Be careful to match the soil correctly.

Narcissus (Daffodil) – upright strappy leaves with yellow and white flowers in late winter and early spring. Poeticus or Pheasant's eye are attractive with flat white petals and rich yellow centres edged in red. They are shade tolerant and many are scented.

Scilla – short strap-like leaves and spikes of starry lavender-blue flowers in early spring. Tolerant of damp and shade.

Tulipa – wonderful goblet-shaped flowers on upright stems throughout spring. Great variations of flower shape and colour.

Summer bulbs

Allium – ornamental onions with wonderful early summer flowers that form globes of purple, pink or white flowers at the end of upright stems. The foliage can be unattractive and floppy but can be hidden by planting among perennials, such as Japanese anamones or cranesbill geraniums, whose new growth will act as a covering. The flowers then appear to float magically in the air.

Convallaria majalis (Lily-of-the-valley) – short lance-shaped leaves with sprays of dainty, fragrant, white flowers in spring. Shade tolerant.

Crocosmia (Montbretia) – tall lance-shaped leaves and brightly coloured funnel-shaped flowers in mid- to late summer.

Fritillaria – grassy leaves and delicate drooping flowers in midsummer, with unusual chequerboard patterns in reds, greens and browns. Tolerant of damp and shade.

Gladiolus – tall strappy leaves and showy spires of funnel-shaped flowers in summer. There are also light, delicate varieties cuch as *G. communis* subsp. *byzantinus.*

Lilium (Lily) – tall stems with lance-shaped leaves and showy summer flowers in reds, oranges, yellows and white.

Autumn bulbs

Cyclamen – low, flat, rounded leaves which often have silvery patterns on a dark green base. Small, upright, carmine, pink or white flowers at varying times depending on the species. Shade tolerant.

Dahlia – tall plants with amazing flower heads in late summer through to autumn in every shape and most colours. Brilliantly coloured or garish according to your viewpoint.

Nerine – small lily-like flowers in crimson, pink and white in autumn. Not hardy.

Biennials

This is a comparatively small group but it does contain many of the loveliest and most useful garden plants. Biennials establish their roots and leaves in the first year, and then flower and set seed in the second. Some are technically perennials but make better garden plants when grown as biennials. You can grow them from seed or buy them as young plants. Treat them as you would a perennial, staking and watering as necessary. Below is a list of the plants most commonly grown as biennials.

Biennial plants

Alcea (Hollyhock) – this is a perennial and if it settles happily in your garden you will get several years' growth from it. They are tall plants with rounded, slightly hairy, leaves. Flowers grow up the stem throughout summer and come in a wide range of colours from white through pinks and yellows to a purply-maroon so deep it almost looks black.

Dianthus barbatus (Sweet William) – this is a perennial that does better as a biennial. In late spring and early summer the clumps of fine leaves are topped with flattish clusters of small sweet-smelling flowers in pinks and white.

Digitalis purpurea (Foxglove) – tall biennial (or perennial if it is happy) with spires of purple, white or apricot flowers in early summer. If you are lucky they will seed themselves and you will find your plants are regularly replenished.

Erysimum cheiri (Wallflower) – these are the perfect match for tulips in spring. Wallflowers grow into small bushy plants that look good all winter. They then flower at the same time as tulips in a wide range of reds and oranges and afterwards they hide the tulips' fading leaves which tend to look unattractive.

Lunaria annua (Honesty) – this is an annual but produces better flowers and seed pods if it has a good start the previous year. It has attractively toothed leaves, and purple or white flowers up and down its stems in early summer. These turn into round, papery seed pods which will remain on the plant right up to winter.

Myosotis (Forget-me-not) – low carpeting plant with hairy leaves and dainty spring flowers in blue, white or pink. These look lovely under tulips. Strictly speaking they are short-lived perennials but once settled they self-seed prolifically and you will find your garden full of them. Some people will not grow them for this reason but they are so charming (and easy to pull up) that this seems a short-sighted approach.

Oenothera biennis (Evening primrose) – tall stems covered with fragrant bowl-shaped flowers throughout summer. The yellow flowers open fully in the evening and seem to light up the garden.

Onorpordum acanthium (Scotch thistle) – a spectacular plant with spiky grey-green leaves and thistle-like flower heads surrounded by spiny bracts. Beware as they can grow large.

Annuals

Annuals germinate, grow, flower, set seed and die within one year, often much less. You may find that some plants, such as snapdragons (*Antirrhinum*) and tobacco plants (*Nicotiana*) which are referred to as annuals last more then a year. This is because they are actually perennials but usually perform better if grown as an annual. By the second year they may become straggly and not flower so well.

Annuals are often referred to as 'bedding plants' as they are usually grown from seed in greenhouses or nursery beds and then moved to their final position as small plants. You can either grow your own from seed or buy small plants.

All annuals (including perennials grown as annuals) are divided into two groups according to their hardiness:

1 Hardy plants will survive frost and can be sown directly outside where they will flower. Many, such as love-in-a-mist (*Nigella*) and sweet peas (*Lathyrus odoratus*) can be sown the previous autumn for larger plants and earlier flowering. Many will self-seed and come up again in subsequent years.
2 Half-hardy plants cannot be planted out until the risk of frost has passed. Most also need a temperature of 10 °C/50 °F to germinate. For this reason the seeds need to be started off under glass but a warm window sill will do just as well as a greenhouse.

Annuals are very easy to look after but because their life cycle is so short they have some requirements which you cannot ignore.

- Most annuals need sun, and only busy Lizzies (*Impatiens*) and tobacco plants (*Nicotiana*) will do well in deep shade.
- Many annuals grow fast – sunflowers (*Helianthus annus*) will reach over 2 m/6 ft, and need support right from the start. If you let tall annuals flop and fall they will grow crooked or even die if their stems are damaged. They grow so quickly that they need to get it right the first time.
- Most annuals need regular supplies of water. This is especially important for plants in containers and hanging baskets which can dry out very quickly.
- Many annuals will flower better if you regularly feed them with an organic supplement such as tomato food. This will encourage the plant to produce more blooms over a longer period and the supplement can easily be added to their water.

- Many annuals need deadheading regularly if you want them to flower throughout the summer.

All this may make it seem as if annuals are difficult to grow but they are very useful and do give a lot in return for a little care.

- Annuals will fill in gaps while slower growing shrubs become established. Big plants like sunflowers (*Helianthus annus*) will fill spaces, and sweet peas (*Lathyrus odoratus*) or even runner beans will attractively cover a blank fence quickly.
- Annuals will provide almost instant colour and can be used to extend the interest in a bed.
- As annuals are short-lived you can vary your display each year.
- Annuals are ideal for containers as they can be used to create year-round colour and interest. A pot with a shrub in it can have a succession of annuals planted around the base which will do the main plant no harm and keep the pot looking good long before or after the shrub has flowered.
- Annuals come in a large variety of shapes, sizes and colours so there is something for everyone. Many are also sweetly scented and a selection of these is listed below.

Fragrant annual plants

Heliotropium – usually grown as an annual with hairy leaves and clusters of tiny purple flowers in summer, which are often fragrant, sometimes unusually so; *H. arborescens* 'Marine' smells of cherry pie and *H. a.* 'Princess Marina' is marzipan scented!

Lathyrus odoratus (Sweet pea) – annual climber with flowers which will continue all summer as long as you pick or deadhead them. Be careful to choose fragrant varieties such as *L. o.* 'Cupani', *L. o.* 'Matucana' or *L. o.* 'Painted Lady'.

Malcomia maritima (Virginia stock) – low-growing annual covered with red or purple flowers throughout summer.

Matthiola (Gillyflower/Stock) – short-lived perennial but often grown as an annual with short spires of fragrant red, pink or white flowers in summer. *M. longipetala* subsp. *bicornis* (Night-scented stock) is especially fragrant at night.

Reseda odorata (Mignonette) – bushy annual with clusters of creamy-green or reddish-green flowers from summer to early autumn.

Climbers

The term 'climbers' covers a great range of plants, crossing all the boundaries between shrubs, perennials and annuals. There is a climber to suit most requirements and the main points to consider are as follows.

- Climbers can be evergreen or deciduous.
- Annual and perennial climbers may die down in winter.
- Some climbers, such as ivy (*Hedera*), are self-clinging and need no support, while others, such as summer jasmine (*Jasminum officinale*), twine themselves around the supports. Clematis and many others hold on with small tendrils.
- Most climbers will not harm the surface beneath them but ivy (*Hedera*) and Virginia creeper (*Parthenocissus*) may cause problems if the surface is already in poor condition. This is worth being aware of when planting climbers against old houses or walls.
- Several non-climbing shrubs can be trained to climb to a certain height by a combination of tying in and pruning.
- Annual climbers are particularly useful for filling a gap temporarily while a slower one grows up.
- Many climbers, such as winter jasmine (*Jasminum nudiflorum*) and most roses, have long stiff stems which regularly need tying in.
- Some plants, such as vines (*Vitis*), climb neatly and will provide a tidy covering for a wall while others, such as honeysuckle (*Lonicera*), scramble all over the place and are perfect for hiding tanks, sheds and any other eyesores.

All climbers need a support. It is much better to fix the structure to be climbed in place first and then plant suitable climbers around it. You must ensure that any structure will be strong enough to support the plant when it is fully grown. Wisterias, Chilean potato plant (*Solanum crispum*) and climbing hydrangea (*H. anomala* subsp. *petiolaris*) all eventually develop large, thick and heavy stems that need sturdy support.

- Wire netting can be fixed to walls or fences using U-staples.
- Trellis can be fixed in front of walls or fences, or above them to give extra height. Position the trellis with the vertical batons next to the wall and the horizontal ones in front so you can fix the plant ties to them. For a more open framework you can put vine eyes (screws with loops at their heads) at intervals and thread wire between them. Always use galvanized fittings that will not rust.

- Many climbers can be trained through trees, shrubs and hedges to provide extra interest. Make sure the flowering times are compatible and that the climber will not grow too big and swamp its host.

You need to choose carefully if you are planting more than one climber in an area. If possible you should try to stagger the flowering or fruiting times to extend the season of interest, but you also need to consider the pruning times; it is difficult to prune a climber if it is intertwined with another plant that is just coming into flower. Below are a few useful climbers.

Deciduous climbers

These will provide a good screen in summer and may let more light into the garden in winter.

Actinidia kolomikta – deciduous climber with pink, green and white variegated leaves. Fragrant cup-shaped flowers in summer are followed on female plants by oblong fruits. Needs full sun.

Campsis (Trumpet vine) – vigorous, deciduous climber with orangy-scarlet, trumpet-shaped flowers in summer and autumn. Tolerant of dry soil and wind. Happy in sun or shade.

Hydrangea anomala subsp. *petiolaris* (Climbing hydrangea) – big deciduous climber with creamy-white flowers in summer. Tolerant of dry soil and shade.

Jasminum nudiflorum (Winter jasmine) – yellow flowers along the arching stems in winter are followed by pale green leaves. The long stems have a tendency to flop and need to be regularly tied into a supporting framework. Tolerant of dry soil and shade.

Lathyrus latifolius (Perennial pea) – perennial with bluey-green leaves and pinky-purple unscented flowers from summer to autumn. Likes sun or part shade.

Parthenocissus (Virginia creeper) – rampant, deciduous climber which turns beautiful shades of red and orange in autumn. Happy in sun or shade.

Tropaeoleum speciosum (Scottish flame flower) – perennial with delicate stems perfect for twining through a host shrub. In summer, the stems are turned into garlands with small, bright red, long-spurred flowers all along them. Towards autumn the flowers turn into turquoise blue berries with the red calyces remaining. Likes sun or part shade.

Vitis (Vine) – deciduous climber with tiny green flowers in summer followed by edible fruits in autumn. *V. coignetiae* has huge leaves which turn bright red in autumn. Happy in sun or shade. *V.* 'Brandt' produces edible blue-black fruits and *V. vinifera* produces wine grapes. Both need full sun.

Wisteria – vigorous deciduous climber with showy panicles of blue, violet or white flowers in early summer. Needs full sun.

Semi-evergreen climbers

Some of these climbers may remain evergreen in mild winters, others may vary according to the species.

Akebia quinata (Chocolate vine) – semi-evergreen with leaves which are pale green above, bluey-green below, and develop a purple hue in winter. The purply-brown spring flowers are spicily scented and are followed by long seed pods. Happy in sun or shade.

Clematis 1 – early-flowering species. These have small flowers in winter and early spring and like their roots in shade and their tops in sun. *C. armandii* and *C. cirrhosa* are evergreen, *C. alpina*, *C. macropetala* and *C. montana* are deciduous and hardier.

Clematis 2 – large-flowered cultivars. These are deciduous and flower in late spring or early summer and again in autumn. They also like their roots in shade and their tops in sun. Many named varieties.

Clematis 3 – late-flowering group, including large-flowered cultivars, small-flowered cultivars and species. These flower in late summer and early autumn and can have attractive seed heads. The species include *C. tangutica* and *C. viticella*, which are shade tolerant and largely resistant to clematis wilt which can kill other varieties. Happy in sun or shade.

Jasminum officinale (Summer jasmine) – semi-evergreen with small, pinky-white, fragrant flowers in summer. Tolerant of dry soil. Needs full sun.

Lonicera (Honeysuckle) – scrambling semi-evergreen with clusters of fragrant tubular flowers. The flowers range from cream to red, mixed with all shades of yellow and pink and blossom in winter or summer, depending on the species. Likes sun or part shade.

Solanum crispum (Chilean potato vine) – fast-growing, semi-evergreen with lilacy-blue flowers throughout summer. *S. jasminoides* has bluey-white flowers. Needs full sun.

Evergreen climbers

These will provide a solid layer throughout the year.

Hedera (Ivy) – it may seem as if ivy is everywhere, and it will survive almost any conditions and is a good year-round backdrop. The leaves can vary from dark green to almost blue or purple. Yellow or white variegated forms are available. Tolerant of any soil and any aspect.

Trachelospermum jasminoides (Star jasmine) – evergreen with glossy green leaves which turn reddy-brown in winter. Fragrant white flowers in mid- to late summer. Wind tolerant. Likes sun or part shade.

For roses, see page 62.

Shrubs as climbers

A number of bush shrubs can be trained as climbers and will successfully grow up a support to about 3 m/10 ft. Californian lilac (*Ceanothus*), flowering quince (*Chaenomeles*), cotoneaster, spindle (*Euonymus*), forsythia and pyracantha are a few examples. Buy a fairly small plant and tie it gently but firmly in place right from the start. Tie the branches in regularly as they grow, removing older ties once the plant has shaped correctly. You can also use the yearly prune to make any necessary corrections. Bear in mind it will be almost impossible to retrain an established plant.

Annual climbers

You can either plant these every year or use them as a temporary measure to provide a quick covering. They look their best from midsummer until the first frosts.

Cobaea scandens (Cup and saucer plant) – this is an evergreen perennial but is tender and usually grown as an annual. From summer until autumn it is covered with long, fragrant, bell-shaped flowers that open creamy-white and fade to purple.

Ipomoea tricolor (Morning glory) – a fast-growing annual or tender perennial which rapidly twines up any support. Throughout the summer it is covered with a succession of funnel-shaped flowers in blue, white or crimson that open in the morning sunlight and than fade as evening draws in.

Lathyrus odoratus (Sweet pea) – a hardy annual that is best scrambling up a trellis or free-standing tepee of poles. Sweetly scented flowers will grow all summer as long as you deadhead or pick them regularly.

Runner beans – these are easily grown from seed and will quickly twine up supports. The flowers are red or white and you have the added bonus of beans to eat later in the summer.

Tropaeolum majus (Nasturtium) – this has rounded leaves with wavy edges and slightly funnel-shaped flowers with long spurs. The flowers will continue throughout summer into autumn and come in all shades from creamy yellow through orange to deep red.

Lawns and meadows

The accepted wisdom is that if you have a very small garden, a damp one or a shady one, you should not attempt to have a lawn as it will never thrive, and if you want to help the environment, lawns require too much water and mowers cause pollution. The mistake here is to confuse fine lawn with roughly cut grass that you can lie on, walk through in bare feet and use to play on. Fine lawns with immaculate stripes are hard work to maintain and are wasteful due to the constant watering they require. However, slightly longer, tougher grass will give you all the benefits with none of the waste. You do not have to go as far as growing a meadow (although you could if you wanted) – have a lawn and just leave the grass a little longer and do not be too precious about it.

If you are starting a lawn from scratch, it is worth making sure you get the right type of grass for your requirements. Utility grass contains a percentage of meadow and rye grasses, which are coarse-leaved and tough. They can be allowed to grow slightly longer, which means that you do not have to mow so often and the grass is not put under so much stress. This will give you a perfectly good lawn that will be able to cope with periods of wet and dry reasonably well. Slightly rough grass is the cheapest and usually the easiest way of covering large areas of ground.

Laying a lawn

When you are planning a new lawn remember that:

- lawns need soil that drains well and is not compacted. Light sandy soils should have compost added and heavy clay soils should have sand dug in
- reasonable levels of sunshine are also important; grass that is permanently in deep shade will tend to become thin and straggly
- a lawn will not survive being trampled over regularly, especially when it is wet or frozen. If there is a route you frequently take across your lawn, construct a path or insert stepping stones in the grass.

Seed versus turf

If you are starting to make a lawn, not only do you have to choose the correct type of grass but also you have to decide whether to use seed or turf. There are pros and cons for each.

- Turf can be laid at any time as long as the weather is not too hot, too dry or too frosty. Turf will give you an instant effect and can be walked on quicker than grass grown from seeds. Yet it works out about ten times more expensive than seed. In terms of preparation there is little to choose between the two, although turves are heavy to move when you get around to the actual laying and must be placed within a couple of days of being delivered.
- Seed is much cheaper and easier to use for awkwardly shaped areas. After sowing, the area must be protected from birds who will eat the seeds and cats who will regard the area as a giant litter tray! Both can be deterred by erecting small stakes around the area and running black cotton thread around and across it. The other risk to new seedlings is weeds which will establish themselves, smother the new grass and use up the nutrients in the soil.
- As a rough guideline, turf is usually best for a small area or where you need an instant effect and seeds are better if you want to grass a large area cheaply. In the long run, seeds may also produce a better lawn as you will be able to choose the exact seed mix.

Preparation

It is worth preparing the soil well as this will give you healthy grass which will last longer, look better and need less maintenance.

1 Clear away all weeds, stones and other debris.
2 Dig in compost and sharp sand if the drainage is poor.
3 Level the site. Gentle undulations are fine, but small bumps will ruin the grass every time you mow.
4 Leave it for a month so that you can pull up any weeds that germinate.
5 Choose a fine day, when the soil is not too damp, and then flatten it by 'treading'. This involves walking across the site with your feet close together and taking tiny steps with the pressure on your heels (obviously wearing flat shoes or boots). If you want bulbs in your grass, such as daffodils, crocuses or snowdrops, now is the time to put them in.
6 Once the site is flattened, rake it again and then apply a granular fertilizer according to the manufacturer's instructions.

Sowing seed

Choose the correct seed mix according to your requirements. It is important that you follow the quantities accurately. If you sow the grass too thinly, weeds will grow up in between and if you sow it too thickly, the individual plants will not thrive. If possible you should sow in mid-spring or mid-autumn when the weather is warm to encourage germination.

1 Mark straight edges with posts and string and mark curves with a hose.
2 Put plastic sheeting along the edge of the proposed lawn and sprinkle seed so it goes over the plastic; this will ensure the grass grows thickly right up to the edge of the lawn. To ensure you scatter the seed evenly, work out how much seed you need in total and, depending on the size of your plot, divide the area into four or six portions. This will give you a smaller area to scatter over and you are less likely to scatter too thinly or thickly.
3 When you have finished, gently rake over the area to spread a fine covering of soil over the seeds. Then water gently and put up canes with fine twine between them to deter birds and cats.

4 The seed will take about three weeks to grow and should be ready for use after about ten weeks. Do not cut until at least 5 cm/2 in, and water regularly throughout the first growing season.

Laying turf

Be careful when choosing turf. Cheap turves may contain a high percentage of weeds. Also avoid meadow turf unless you want to create a meadow.

1 Prepare the soil following steps shown in 'Preparation' above.
2 The turves should be laid within 48 hours of their arrival. If this is not possible, lay them on plastic or paving, grass side up, in a shady spot and keep well watered.
3 Turf can be laid at any time of year but the soil should be moist rather than wet or dry.
4 When laying turves, stagger the rows and push the edges up close together as the turf may shrink slightly.
5 If you need to add a small piece to complete a row, do it in the middle, rather than at the end and it will be less likely to dry out.
6 If you need to cut curves, lay the whole turf and then mark the curve. You can trim the turves using a spade or half-moon cutter.
7 Once you have laid all the turves, use the back of a rake or a light roller to flatten them and get rid of any air pockets.
8 Turf usually establishes itself more quickly than seeded grass and can be used after about four to six weeks. During this time and after, water well. Turves need more water than seeds as the water has to penetrate right down to the roots.

Maintenance

The type of lawn you have will govern how much care it needs, but all grass needs a certain amount of maintenance.

Mowing

Lawns should be cut regularly, partly to keep them looking neat, but also to prevent weeds and moss establishing themselves. From mid-spring to mid-autumn you should cut the lawn about every seven to ten days, but if the weather is very hot and dry allow the grass to grow longer so it is under less stress. Similarly, in winter leave it slightly longer as a protection against frost. (Pretty as your footprints may look you should avoid walking on frosty grass.) If your grass becomes very long do not cut it right back in one go; it is much less of a shock for the grass if you reduce its height over two or three cuts. The same goes for the first cut of spring, which should only remove the top 1 cm/ ½ in of grass. For information on lawnmowers, see Chapter 06.

Watering

You will need to water new grass while it is establishing itself but after that you should not really water a lawn. If you water your lawn as soon as it is dry the grass will actually become weaker because it will become dependent on a regular supply of water. Even if your grass does turn brown it doesn't really matter, it will green up again as soon as it rains.

Feeding

Most utility lawns will never need feeding. If yours is looking a little unhealthy it can be fed in spring or autumn – use a nitrogen-based feed in spring to encourage growth and a more general feed in autumn. Be careful to select the right feed for your requirements and always follow the manufacturer's instructions as too much can do more harm than good. Most grass is better in the long run if it is not fed because it becomes tougher and less dependent on extra nutrients.

Edging

A neatly edged lawn will automatically look better, even if you leave the grass a little longer. The choice of equipment available to do edging is covered in Chapter 06. You can trim the edges using a half-moon cutter, but remember you are cutting away lawn that will not grow back.

Aerating

If your lawn is used frequently, the soil beneath it can become compacted and will not drain properly. Ideally you should aerate your lawn every three years, but this is probably over-optimistic for most people. Aerating should be carried out in the autumn, after the grass has been cut and when it is neither too wet nor too dry. Use a garden fork or a specially designed aerator which has hollow tines, and push your tool 5 cm/2½ in into the soil. Ease it back and forth, remove and repeat at 15 cm/6 in intervals. The hollow-tined aerator removes small plugs of earth, that can be brushed away later. The holes will improve drainage, allow nutrients to penetrate to the roots, and make moss less likely to grow. Spread top dressing over the lawn (3 kg per sq m/6 lb per sq yd). A good mix for top dressing is half well-rotted garden compost or leaf mould and half sand. This will feed your lawn and improve its general health. Brush it into the holes but do not worry if some of the dressing remains visible. As long as it is only a thin layer and is below the level of the tips of the grass it will do no harm and will soon sink down. If your lawn has bare patches you can add grass seed as well.

Scarifying

With time, thatch can develop at the base of the grass stems. This is a mixture of dead and living organic matter, and if it gets too thick it can prevent water, air and nutrients penetrating the soil. The grass will gradually become weaker and more prone to disease. To remove thatch, choose an autumn day when the soil is moist and rake the lawn over using a spring-tined rake (see Chapter 06). Apply a top dressing afterwards and be warned that the lawn will actually look worse when you have finished! The full benefits will not be apparent until the new growth comes up in the spring.

Sweeping

You should always sweep any fallen leaves from your lawn as they will quickly become a soggy mat and prevent air and light reaching the grass.

Weeding

According to your viewpoint, daisies and buttercups may be charming additions to your lawn or highly invasive weeds. The best way, if you have a small lawn, is to dig each weed out by hand as it appears. A good method, particularly for dandelions which have deep roots, is to dig vertically around the plant with an old kitchen knife. Lever the knife so you can remove the plug of earth surrounding the weed, being careful to remove the entire root otherwise it will simply regrow. If you have a large area of grass it really isn't worth worrying about a few weeds. The presence of moss is more serious because it means your lawn is not in good condition. Lack of aeration, too much or too little water, too much shade or lack of nutrients in the soil can all be causes of moss. Prevention is better than cure and if you follow the steps above your grass should be healthy enough to withstand moss. If it really is a problem, it might be worth considering a tougher ground-cover plant from the lists below.

Lawn plants

Chamaemelum nobile (Chamomile) – this needs full sun and well-drained soil. Once established it will suppress weeds and only need occasional trimming. *C. n.* 'Treneague' does not flower but is very fragrant and gives the best cover.

Mentha requienii (Creeping Corsican mist) – this is suitable for damp shady areas. It provides good cover, has attractive purple flowers, and can be walked on a little but dies back in winter.

Thymus (Thyme) – this needs full sun and well-drained soil. The prostrate varieties *T. polytrichus* or *T. serpyllum* provide the best cover. Both are fragrant and flower in summer but, be warned, they attract large numbers of bees so you need to be careful when walking on or near the plants.

The traditional enemies of moss and clover can also be used to create small lawns.

Ground-cover plants

Depending on the situation and the use of the area, there are a number of plants that can be used to create non-grass lawns or areas of slightly taller ground cover. Non-grass lawns will usually only cope with a small amount of traffic and will probably need hand weeding until the plants are established. For these reasons they are best suited to fairly small areas.

Ground-cover plants do exactly what they say and cover the ground. They thereby prevent weeds and fill an area that you don't want to devote too much time to but, equally, that you don't want full of weeds. Be careful as many ground-cover plants tend to be invasive and can take over the garden and become weeds themselves.

Ground-cover plants for sun

Aubrietia – evergreen, carpet-forming perennial with small pink or purple flowers in spring.

Erigeron karvinskianus – perennial with grey-green foliage and daisy flowers throughout the summer that start white and turn pink as they age.

Saponaria ocymoides (Tumbling Ted) – perennial with hairy green leaves and an abundance of little pink flowers in summer.

Stachys byzantina (Rabbits' ears) – mat-forming perennial with soft, woolly, greeny-white leaves. In summer there are spires of woolly purple flowers.

Ground-cover plants for shade

Ajuga reptans (Bugle) – evergreen perennial with upright spires of dark blue flowers in late spring and early summer.

Hosta – evergreen perennial with decorative lance- or heart-shaped leaves in varying shades of greens and blues. Small bell-shaped flowers in shades of lavender in summer are more abundant if there is some light.

Omphalodes cappadocica – clump-forming, semi-evergreen perennial with dainty blue and white flowers in spring.

Pachysandra terminalis – spreading evergreen perennial with glossy dark green leaves and spikes of little white flowers in early summer.

Pulmonaria – low-growing perennial with hairy, attractively mottled leaves. Small spring flowers come in shades of pink, purple, blue or all three.

Ground-cover plants for any position

Alchemilla mollis – hummocky perennial with crinkly leaves that look lovely with raindrops on them. Tiny greenish-yellow flowers in summer.

Campanula – low-growing varieties of this perennial form good ground cover and have cup- or bell-shaped blue or purple flowers in summer. *C. carpactica*, *C. cochlearifolia* (Fairies' thimbles), *C. portenschalagiana*, and *C. poscharskyana* are all suitable.

Hedera helix (Ivy) – small-leaved ivies provide good year-round cover.

Persicaria affinis – mat-forming evergreen perennial with little spires of pink or red flowers in summer which turn brown in winter.

Vinca minor (Periwinkle) – low-growing evergreen shrub with bluey-purple or white propeller-like flowers from spring to autumn. They flower best given reasonable light levels.

Meadows

Meadows are quick to create because they contain a high percentage of annuals, but they are hard to maintain as the delicate balance of plants can easily be disrupted. It is important to remember that most meadow plants flourish on relatively poor soil.

To make a meadow from an existing grassy area, stop mowing and introduce traditional, robust, wild flowers. Depending on the size of the area and your budget you can use plug plants or seeds. Whatever you do, don't dig up wild plants but try to source local species as they will naturalise more easily. To create a meadow from scratch is often easier in the long run as you can replicate the poor soil which meadows thrive on naturally.

- In the autumn remove any grass or plants, taking away about 10–15 cm/4–6 in of soil at the same time. This is likely to be the most fertile and may be too rich for your meadow.
- Break up the soil below and remove any weeds such as dock or thistle. It may seem strange to weed an area that is going to be left wild but while it is getting established your meadow will need tending to ensure that the wrong sort of plants don't take over.
- In spring gently flatten the soil as you would for planting grass (see page 78).
- You can now plant plugs or scatter seed. In practice a mixture of the two is usually best with the plugs 15–20 cm/6–8 in apart and the seeds in between.
- Meadow seed mixes are easy to buy and will give you a good balance of plants. They are available for different soils and come in a range of colours (pastel, bright, etc.). Typical plants are poppies (*Papaver*), love-in-a-mist (*Nigella*), campion (*Silene*), cornflower (*Centaurea*) and meadow cranesbill (*Geranium pratense*).
- Rye grass (*Lolium*) seeds are useful for filling gaps.
- Yellow rattle (*Rhinathus minor*) is also a useful annual plant to help maintain the balance of plants in your meadow. It germinates at exactly the same time as many of the stronger grasses start to grow and takes much of their water and nutrients, thereby preventing them from becoming too rampant. Luckily it is an attractive plant in its own right with pretty yellow flowers and rattly seed heads.

For the first few years you will need to check that the balance in your meadow is correct, pulling up species which are too invasive and replacing plants as necessary. After that maintenance is fairly easy.

- In late summer or early autumn cut back to about 30 cm/12 in using shears or a strimmer.
- Cut in straight lines to allow the resident wildlife time to escape, if possible leaving an area uncut each year for them to

live in. This only needs to be a relatively small area at the edge and can be rotated each year.

- Rake the grass up and leave to dry if you want hay or compost straight away.
- Then cut with a mower on a high setting to remove any clippings, and rake with a spring-tined rake (see Chapter 06) to remove any thatch. The grass clippings will rot down and make the soil too rich and both they and the thatch will hinder the germination of seeds for the following year.

tools

In this chapter you will learn:

- **the basic tools every gardener needs and how to use them**
- **how to work out which specialist tools you may require.**

Introduction

Depending on the sort of gardener you are and the kind of garden that you have, you will find some of the tools mentioned in this chapter invaluable and others you will have no use for whatsoever. You will almost certainly need a trowel, a watering can and a pair of secateurs, but otherwise it is better to wait until you actually need a particular tool before buying it. It is all too easy to find yourself superbly kitted out with a range of expensive tools that you never use.

There is a vast array of gardening tools on the market. When buying your tools, choose carefully and bear in mind that on the whole the price will reflect the quality and the length of service you will get. Stainless steel tools cost much more than ordinary steel, but they do not rust and are easy to use. Coated steel is much cheaper and lasts reasonably well if kept clean. Good tools are essential if you are going to use them a lot. For less frequent use, you will probably do just as well with a cheaper model.

Make sure that the tool is the right size for you and that you can use it comfortably. Spades and forks in particular must be the correct height for you.

Types of tools

Trowel

This is the most essential tool and is useful for planting everything except large shrubs and trees. As you will use it often, it is worth buying a good stainless steel model with a comfortable wooden handle. Trowels are available in various shapes and sizes, for example, narrow-bladed trowels (5 cm/2 in) are particularly useful for small annuals and bulbs.

Hand fork

Hand forks are useful for weeding and breaking up small areas of soil. Flat tines (prongs) are the most efficient to use. Buy the best and strongest you can afford (roots of plants can be very hard to dig up) and choose the length of handle that you find most comfortable. Short handles give you more control, but long-handled forks will reach further.

Spade

You will need a spade unless you only garden in containers, and even then you may find one useful for transferring compost. Spades come in various heights and widths and it is vital that you get one that is comfortable to use. The handles are in the shape of a T, Y or D. The T shape can be tiring to use, but the choice is really up to you (see Figure 6.1).

The blades come in various shapes and sizes and must be sharp to slide easily through the soil. As with all tools, stainless steel ones are the best, particularly for heavy clay soils. Most blades are flat-bottomed but some are curved or pointed. Larger blades will obviously shift more soil but are much heavier to use both as an implement and because of the amount of soil they will displace. Smaller spades are called 'border spades' because they are more manageable for use in a planted border.

Two points to check when buying a spade:

- Check that the socket fixing the blade to the handle is strong.
- Check that there is a tread along the top of the blade. This protects the soles of your shoes and gives you a better grip.

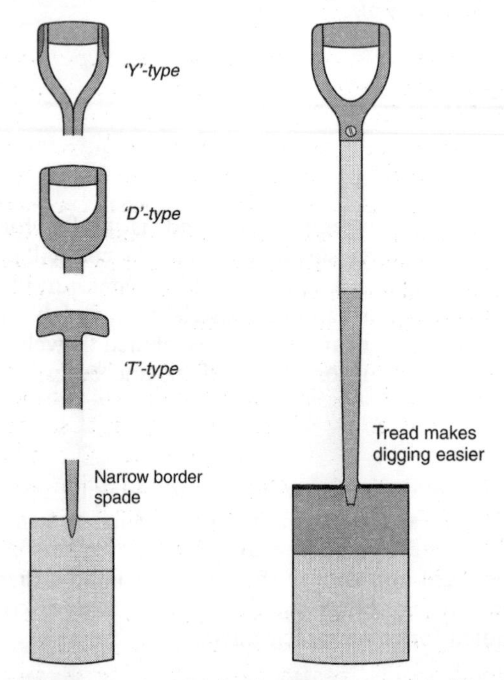

figure 6.1 standard and border spades with tread at the top of the blade. Y-, D- and T-type handles

Fork

Many people prefer to use a fork as their main digging tool because they break up soil and dig up plants or weeds without splitting the roots. They come in various sizes and may have flat or rounded tines (prongs), both of which work well. Match the tool to the amount of work you need to do and to your comfort.

Secateurs

Secateurs must be easy and comfortable to use and they must be as sharp as possible so as not to damage the plant while cutting it. They should be able to cut up to 1 cm/½ in diameter effortlessly. Check that you can grip the handles without difficulty while wearing gardening gloves, that you can put the safety catch on and off with the same hand, and that you can still hold them easily when they are fully opened. The blades can be either straight or curved. Straight or anvil secateurs do not always make such a neat cut. Quality is really important with secateurs, so buy the best ones that you can afford.

Equipment for watering

Whether you have a small balcony or a large country estate, you will find that you need a watering can. Much of your watering can probably be done by a hose, but the jet is often too strong for seedlings and young plants and it is hardly worth hauling the hose through to the front of the house to water two window boxes. Watering cans are available in plastic or metal and for most people the 10 litre/2 gallon size is manageable. Ideally it should have a choice of roses (spout ends) to give you a fine or heavy spray. Make sure you are able to carry it with one hand comfortably when it is full of water.

If your garden is larger than a small patio, it is well worth buying a hose and, if possible, installing an outdoor tap. You also need to think about where to store your hose when it is not in use. Hose reels are best for this purpose and can be mounted on a wall. A variety of nozzles is available, but all you really need is one that will adjust from a single jet to a fine spray. Finally, make sure you buy a hose long enough to reach all parts of your garden.

Sprinklers may seem an efficient and easy way of watering a large area, but in fact most of the water evaporates before it can do any good. Sprinklers also waste a lot of water on areas, such as garden paths, that do not need a good soaking.

Simple hand sprayers which hold half to one litre (one to two pints) of water are useful either for spraying a gentle mist over small plants or treating pests. Keep separate sprayers for these different purposes and label each carefully.

Pruning saw

This is used for cutting branches that are too large for secateurs to deal with. The most useful is called a 'Grecian saw' and has a curved blade with deeply serrated teeth along the inner side. It cuts as you pull it towards you.

Loppers

These are long-handled secateurs that can be used to cut branches that ordinary secateurs could not manage or reach. In practice, if you have ordinary secateurs and a pruning saw, it is unlikely you will need loppers as well. The long handles enable you to reach higher branches, but they can be unwieldy to use.

Shears

These are primarily designed for trimming hedges, but they can be used for cutting small awkward areas of grass around trees, etc. and even for pruning. They should be comfortable to use and not too heavy.

Electric hedge trimmer

This is only worth buying if you have a lot of hedge. A blade 44 cm/18 in long will be enough for most hedges. Trimmers can be extremely dangerous to use so before you buy one check the safety mechanisms – it should have a hand guard and an automatic cut-off if you let go of the trigger. Bear in mind that trimmers are tiring to use and very noisy and will not contribute at all to your peaceful afternoon pottering in the garden (or to your neighbour's!).

Lawnmower

The extent of the grassy areas of your garden will determine what type of lawnmower you need. Anything up to about 75 m^2/ 250 sq ft can be tackled with a simple cylinder mower that you can push yourself. Any more than this and you will need an electrical or petrol mower. Hover mowers adapt best to uneven ground. Cylinder mowers have a series of blades arranged around a cylinder, which cut against a fixed blade at the bottom and give a close cut. Rotary motors have a single blade that turns around, cutting the grass as it turns. These are most suited to dealing with longer grass but can be used for lawns provided you are not aiming at an absolutely flat surface. If in doubt, buy a smaller mower rather than a larger one. Although it will take slightly longer to cut the grass, it will be much easier to manoeuvre.

Strimmers

These are useful for very long grass, for example, meadow areas or around hedges and trees where a mower would be awkward to use. They are powered by petrol or electricity; although the electric ones are much lighter, the length of the cable can be restrictive.

Edgers

If you want your lawn to look neat and tidy where it meets paths and flowerbeds, you will need some sort of edging tool. Long-handled shears are useful for cutting grass that overhangs the edge of the lawn, and cutters with blades at right angles to the handles will trim the grass near the edges. A half-moon cutter will tidy the lawn and can be used to reshape it.

Rakes

A useful general purpose rake is usually about 30 cm/12 in wide with 12 metal teeth, either flattened or circular like large nails. This can be used to collect up stones from the surface and to break up lumps of soil. If you then turn the rake over, it can serve to level the soil.

A spring-tined or wire rake has a curved head and is mostly used on lawns, either to collect leaves or to scratch out moss. The teeth or tines are much finer than on other rakes and will not damage the grass so much (see Figure 6.2).

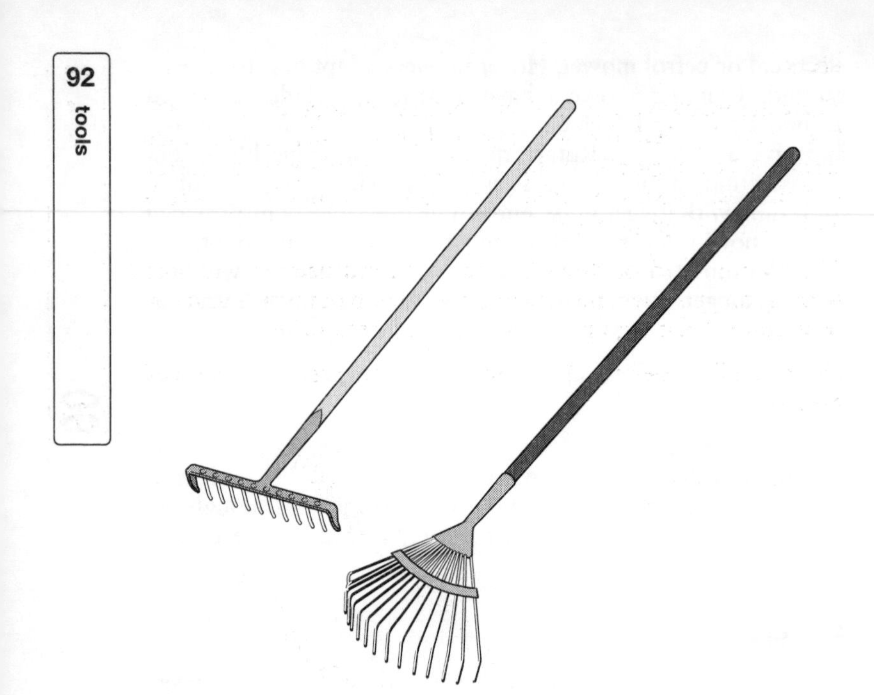

figure 6.2 garden and spring-tined rakes

Besom or brush

A besom is one of the best tools to use for sweeping up leaves and is simply a collection of twigs tied to a larger stick to form a traditional witch's broomstick.

Wheelbarrow

As with many tools, whether or not you need a wheelbarrow will depend on the size of your garden. Most wheelbarrows have a single wheel at the front and two metal legs at the back. Plastic wheelbarrows are lighter to use but not as strong as metal ones. Galvanized metal is probably the most popular material for general use, but you must watch for any rust and treat it as soon as it appears. If you need to push the barrow across the lawn or soft ground frequently, it might be worth buying a ball wheelbarrow or one with an inflatable tyre as this will not sink into the ground so much.

Hoe

There are many types of hoe, but the best all-rounder is a Dutch hoe. This is ideal for weeding in between plants and even seedlings (see Figure 6.3). By pushing the blade parallel to the soil and just below the surface, the blade will cut off any weeds and avoid disrupting the soil.

The swan-necked or draw hoe has a curved neck and is used with an up and down movement. It will chop out weeds and can be used for breaking up soil and drawing seed drills.

Short-handled hoes are also available and are useful in restricted areas.

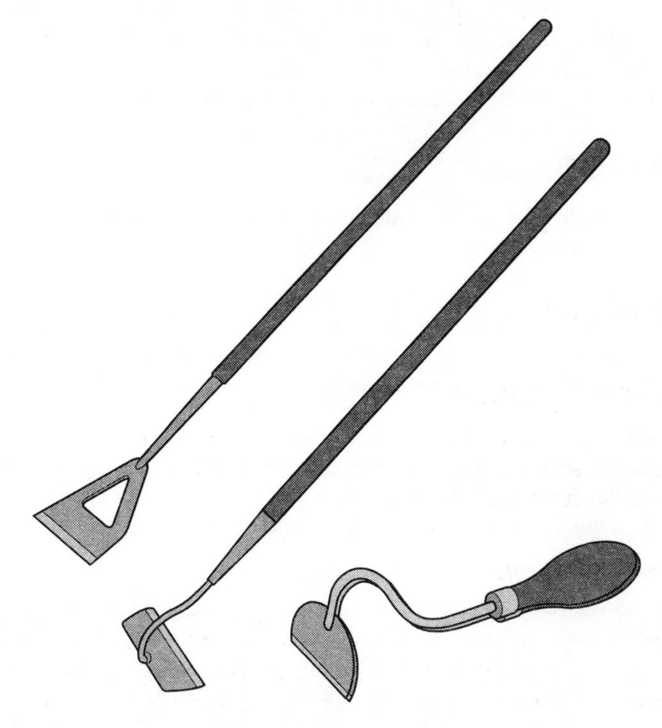

figure 6.3 Dutch, draw and short-handled hoe

Mattock

This is like a small pickaxe, with a sharp, pointy front and a wider chisel-shaped end. It is useful for breaking up stony ground.

Bulb planter

This is useful as it makes a neater hole than a trowel. However, it will only work in medium to heavy soils as sandy soils do not hold together. Bulb planters do not work well in stony soils.

Sieve

Sieves are useful for removing stones from seedbeds and for scattering a fine layer of compost over seeds.

Equipment for seed growing

For this you will need seed trays or plugs, flowerpots, a dibber for making holes and a widger for moving seedlings (the last two can really be improvised by using a pencil and a lolly stick). You will also need a waterproof marker and labels.

Miscellaneous

This section covers the odds and ends that you will almost certainly need.

Gloves

These are a priority unless you have extremely tough hands. They should come well up your wrist. Although they may seem unwieldy, those with suede patches give more protection.

Knife

All professional gardeners insist that you should have a folding knife. Until you get the hang of using one though, it is easy to damage plants. A pair of scissors or secateurs works just as well.

Canes

Bamboo and wooden canes in varying sizes are needed to support some plants. If you do not like the look of bamboo canes, you can paint them green or use natural twigs and branches instead. The sharp tops of canes are very dangerous for your eyes so always put a plastic top or cork on them for protection.

String

Garden string or ties are essential for fixing your plants to supports. Always make sure that you tie the plants loosely enough to allow them to grow. Soft green string does not last as long as plastic ties, but it is gentler for plants.

Bucket

An ordinary bucket can be very useful. You can carry compost in it, soak potted plants in it, use it as a mini wheelbarrow when you are weeding and store your tools in it.

Trug

Trugs are flattish wooden baskets traditionally used for collecting fruit, vegetables and flowers and for holding small tools. Authentic ones are made from split chestnut and willow and may seem expensive but last a long time and age beautifully. Try to get into the habit of putting your tools back into whatever container you use the minute you finish with them as it is surprisingly easy to lose tools even in a small garden.

Shed

You will need somewhere to store your tools when they are not in use. Small upright sheds are useful and can easily be disguised by climbing plants. If you decide to have a shed, buy one that is as large as possible as you will soon accumulate a surprising number of gardening accessories. When choosing it, take care to make it a feature of the garden, rather than an eyesore. Seats with lids are available for storage, but don't just throw your tools in and leave them in a damp rusting heap – clean them first.

Care

Always clean your tools after use. Mud and grass should be wiped off, the metal parts dried and, ideally, non-stainless steel tools wiped with an oily rag. If possible, hang your tools up – this makes them easy to find and also prevents them from becoming damp and rusty.

07 techniques

In this chapter you will learn:

- **where to buy plants and what to look for**
- **how to give your plants the best start**
- **how to keep your garden healthy**
- **propagation or how to get plants for free.**

Introduction

Described below are the various techniques that you will find useful, if not essential, when you start gardening. Although these instructions may seem daunting, in practice plants and gardens are fairly forgiving so do not worry about doing something at exactly the right time or in precisely the right way. Simply follow the general guidelines and give your plants the best possible care you can manage. In the long run, many of these techniques should make life much easier for you. For example, mulching your garden should make weeding unnecessary, cut down on the amount of watering you have to do and enrich your soil, thereby making your plants healthier and stronger.

Preparing the soil

What follows may sound surprising, but you should regard the soil as the most important element in your garden even if it is the most boring to look at. The design of the garden largely depends on you, but the quality of the plants largely depends on the condition of the soil. Before you can put plants into the ground it will probably be necessary to prepare it first. The amount of work you will have to do depends on the state of your garden, but most unplanted areas will benefit from a little tender loving care before you begin to plant anything.

An ideal soil has a deep layer of topsoil with organic matter evenly distributed within it (see Figure 7.1). It retains moisture but does not become waterlogged, has no large stones and is reasonably light and easy to work. In nature, soil like this takes many years to form and very few gardens have an ideal combination. That said, most soils can be improved fairly easily. Most plants grow better if they can send their main roots down deeply, but not many go below 30 cm/12 in. This anchors the plant securely, gives it access to nutrients in the soil and makes it less susceptible to drought.

Traditionally, digging has been regarded as the best way to improve soil quality and, although there is a no-dig method (see page 101) digging is often the best option because it breaks up the soil, allowing roots to grow and water and food to spread through and drain away at the correct rate. When you dig you can also mix in grit, nutrients and organic matter as necessary.

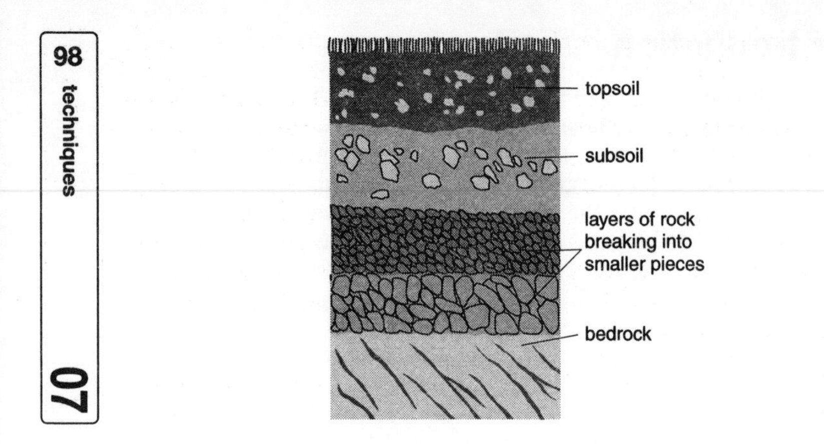

figure 7.1 cross-section of soil showing turf on top, then topsoil and below that subsoil, with the pieces of rock becoming larger towards the bedrock

Digging is not something that you have to do very often. In fact, once the plants are in place you should not dig to any great extent as it will disturb the plants' roots. Kitchen gardens need regular digging in between crops, but elsewhere the only time you usually have to dig seriously is when you are cultivating an area for the first time. Conventionally, in many of the great gardens, all perennials were lifted every three years and the bed dug over, but most people would now regard this as excessive and possibly even harmful.

If you are creating a new bed, the soil will almost certainly be compacted. If you have a new house, builders and machinery will have squashed the soil, and even if you are converting an area of lawn it will have become compacted during its years beneath the grass. If this is the case, roots will not be able to push their way into the soil, water will be unable to penetrate it or will become trapped in pockets, which is worse, and earthworms, the great soil improvers, will be unable to move about easily and break up the soil.

For most soils, digging is best done in autumn when it is damp but not waterlogged. If you find the soil is sticking to your boots, it is too wet to dig. The rain and frost of winter will then break down the clods of earth. Do not dig when the surface has frost on it as this will then be buried beneath the surface and take longer to thaw out.

Digging may seem a simple operation but there is a correct way to do it, and if you use a spade properly you will find the job comparatively easy. The most important fact to remember is to dig as vertically as possible, i.e. keep your back straight, bend your knees and push the spade straight down rather than at an angle. Place one foot on the top of the blade and push down on it using the weight of your body. Pushing with your arms on the handle will achieve less and give you backache sooner. To lift the soil, use your bodyweight to push the handle down thereby raising the blade with the soil on it. As the handle gets lower, bend your knees rather than your back.

If you intend to do a considerable amount of digging, it is worth investing in a good spade. Work out how much you are liable to do and choose the quality of your spade accordingly. If you are only going to put a few plants into an established garden then a cheaper spade will do the job adequately. If you are digging an area with a lot of large stones, such as hardcore, you may need a mattock to break up the soil. However, wherever possible use a spade as the aim of digging is to move soil, not just to break it up. Forks are useful for digging up roots in their entirety whereas a spade will frequently cut through a root and split it.

For large areas, a mechanical rotavator may seem an attractive option as it will quickly turn over a large area of soil and give what appears to be very impressive results for little effort. The drawbacks are that it will not dig as deep as a spade, and if there are perennial weeds it will chop up the roots and spread them around rather than removing them whole.

Single digging is a methodical system which will enable you to improve any area of ground.

Single digging

Small areas of ground can simply be dug over, but the single digging system of trenches allows larger areas to be dug methodically. If you simply dig at random, it is all too easy to miss out some areas and dig others twice.

1 Dig a trench across the area roughly one spit (spade blade) deep and one spit wide (see Figure 7.2).
2 Put the soil from this trench into a barrow and spread it out along the far end of the area to be dug. It will be used to fill the last trench you dig. It is not necessary to break up all the clods of earth as the rain and frost of winter will do it for you.

3 Dig a similar trench alongside the first one, using the soil from the second trench to fill the first.
4 Pick out any roots of perennial weeds that are exposed.
5 A generous amount of organic matter, such as garden compost or well-rotted manure, should be mixed in with the soil as you move it into the trench, preferably spread evenly between the surface and the bottom of the trench as this will encourage the plant roots to grow deep down into the earth. You can also add grit if necessary.
6 Be careful not to tread on the soil you have already dug as you do not want to re-compact it. A plank of wood can be useful to stand on as it will distribute your weight evenly.
7 Move across the plot repeating this procedure until you reach the far side when you can fill the last trench with the soil that came from the first one.

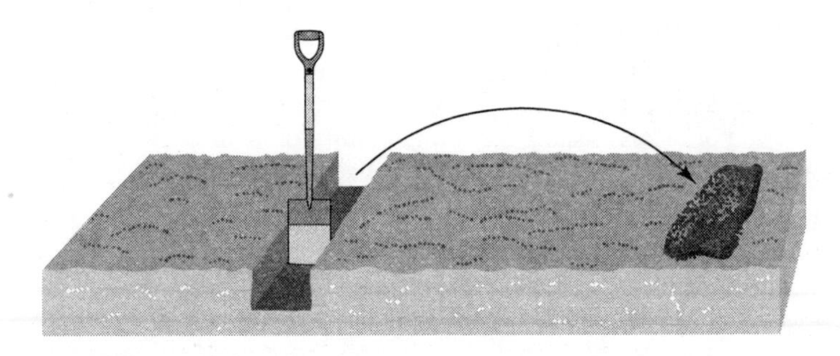

Method for single digging. The soil is moved from the first trench to the end of the site where it will infill the last trench.

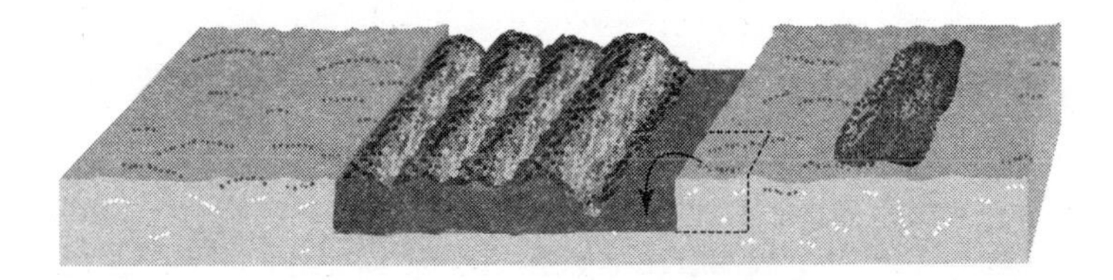

As you work across the site, the soil from each new trench is used to infill the previous one.

figure 7.2

The level of the ground will have risen considerably but this will gradually sink back down as the soil adjusts. Ideally, the soil should then be left over winter to naturally break down and settle. As a minimum leave it for three weeks before planting or sowing. You will then need to level the soil.

1 Choose a day when the soil is dry on top and moist underneath.
2 Push a rake back and forth across the soil, being careful not to dig it in too deeply. If you push away harder than you pull towards yourself, the soil will end up level and the surface debris, such as leaves and twigs, will be caught up un the rake, and can be cleared away without difficulty.
3 Repeat this working across the plot at a right angle. The ground will level out completely and be ready for planting.

No-dig method

There is an alternative system where you can improve the condition of the soil without having to dig. Advocates of this system say that digging is actually harmful to the soil as it disrupts its structure, causes it to dry out more quickly and may expose weed seeds that will then germinate. The argument is that in the wild plants grow perfectly well without the soil being dug and that any treatment necessary can be applied to the surface. This argument is fine as far as it goes, but the problem is that by their very nature gardens are not 'natural'.

If the soil has never been compacted, simply adding organic material to the surface is a perfectly good way to enrich any soil, even heavy clay. The two main points to remember are that at least 5 cm/2 in of organic material should be added to the surface every year and that you must *never* walk on the soil. This makes the system particularly suitable for raised beds or long, narrow beds with walkways in between.

1 Create paths so that you will not need to walk on the growing area. They can be paved, grass, gravel or compacted earth, depending on the amount of use they will get when wet. Trampled earth is the easiest but it will also rapidly become the muddiest. A good compromise is a series of paving stones, large enough to stand or kneel on, placed at regular intervals between the planted areas.
2 Cut down any weeds.

3 Cover the area so no light can get through and allow more weeds to grow. This covering can consist of a thick layer of mulch, black plastic or even old carpeting or cardboard. Ideally this should now be left on for a year to ensure all weeds are eradicated. Obviously this is not a very attractive option but it is highly effective.
4 It is possible to grow certain crops, such as Brussels sprouts, broccoli or squashes, during the waiting time if you have used a porous covering. Either push the mulch away around the plant or cut a hole in the carpet or cardboard. You can also get a specially made black plastic that will allow water through but will block the light and prevent weeds growing.
5 Once the weeds have been eradicated, other plants can be put in or seeds sown. Add more mulch to maintain the soil structure but always clear an area immediately around plants to stop them rotting.

Raised beds

These are useful if your soil is poor, badly drained or if you have difficulty bending. If the soil at the base is very compacted, you will need to break it up first but you can then put a layer of good soil on the top. As long as the bed is 30 cm/12 in deep most plants will not need to penetrate the lower level. You must not step on the soil, so the maximum width of a bed should be 1.5 m/5 ft. Solid timber planks make good edgings, and if they are wide enough you can even use them as kneelers.

The arguments for and against digging can be broadly summarized as follows:

- Digging breaks up badly compacted soils and can quickly improve poor quality ones.
- Digging is hard work, can destroy the soil's existing structure, turn up weeds and is not a process that occurs naturally.
- The no-dig method is slow and the soil needs to be in reasonably good condition.

The state of your garden is likely to decide the method you need to use. If it is in reasonable condition you have the option of either method, but if it is badly compacted you will have to dig.

Buying plants and sundries

Having prepared your garden and decided what you want, you can now go and buy the plants. Plants from a local organic nursery will be environmentally better and probably healthier than mass-produced trays in a supermarket. The more expensive and long-lived your plant is, the more care you need to take. There are a number of different options and, as with everything you need to balance the pros and cons and work out what is best for you:

Specialist nurseries and mail order

Specialist nurseries are the places to go if you want a particular variety of plant or if you are buying a major feature such as a tree. It is best if you can choose the plants yourself but many nurseries offer mail-order services, and if you buy from a reputable nursery the plants should be good. The main snag about mail order is that you have no control over when the plants arrive. Plants do need to be dealt with the minute they come, even if you only roughly heel them in on a spare patch of soil. However, the main advantages of mail order are that you have a wide range of plants to choose from and the plants themselves are usually good value.

Garden centres

This may be the most convenient place to buy your plants. You can choose when you buy them, and everything else you need for your garden should also be available. A quick look around will tell you the quality of the plants. You will not, however, find many specialized plants in your average garden centre and it is likely to be an expensive way to stock your garden.

Flower shows

These can be excellent places to buy plants. Most of the growers will be experts and able to offer good advice. You may not be able to buy plants on the spot but you will be able to see exactly what they look like and then order them. Prices tend to vary so look around before buying anything. Be careful when buying plants that are being sold off cheaply at the end of a show. They may be genuine bargains but they may have had a stressful time at the show and even been forced to flower unnaturally early or late.

Moreovers, you may be tempted to buy something unsuitable – the bougainvillea that looked so splendid at the midsummer show will probably die when exposed to the reality of winter in your garden.

DIY and hardware shops

There is usually only a limited choice available in these shops and the plants may or may not be in good condition. That said, they can be good value, especially for annuals.

Market stalls

These stock a limited range of plants but the plants are usually cheap and can be good quality. Check the plants look healthy before you buy them.

What to look for when buying plants

Having decided where to buy your plants, you need to know what to look for.

Buying trees and shrubs

Bare-rooted – this is often the method used by mail-order nurseries, and many shrubs, particularly roses, do well when transported and then planted out in this state. It is important that this takes place while the plant is dormant, usually between late autumn and early spring. If choosing a bare-rooted plant in a nursery, make sure no buds are open, the stems look healthy and the roots strong with no small white roots growing. The plant should be planted, or at least heeled in, immediately.

Container-grown – the main advantages with container-grown plants are that you can transport the plants easily, wait until you want to put them in the garden, and plant them at almost any time of year. There are a number of points to check before you buy your plants:

- Always make sure the compost is damp and the plant is firmly in the pot. If you lift the plant by the base of the stem and it comes out of the pot easily, this indicates the plant has only just been put in the container and is not a good specimen to buy as it will be unsettling for it to be planted out so soon after re-potting.

- Plants with roots poking out of the bottom of the pot should be avoided as this indicates they have been contained too long and have become pot-bound.
- Check the plants look healthy: firm, unblemished leaves, even growth and plenty of foliage on evergreens are all signs of good health.
- There should be no weeds or moss growing in the pot.
- Choose small specimens rather than large ones as these will settle into your garden much more quickly and grow faster in the long run.

Some plants, especially evergreens, come with their roots and soil wrapped in a ball of hessian or similar material. This usually works well as long as the wrapping has been kept damp and the roots are not growing around in circles inside it.

Buying perennials

Nearly all perennials come in individual pots. Follow the general guidelines for shrubs but bear in mind that many die down in winter and may look unprepossessing at the start of spring. If you buy larger plants, you can often divide them to make more, but ensure the plant is healthy and will divide easily.

Buying bulbs

Bulbs should be firm, free of mould and show slight signs of growth at the top. If you cannot plant them out straight away, store them somewhere cool, dark and dry.

Buying annuals

The main danger here is that many annuals are not frost-hardy and must not be planted out too early. Many of those on display in garden centres early in the season are kept partly under cover or are brought in at night. The time to buy half-hardy annuals is when there is no longer a danger of frost and not when there is a public holiday or an enticing display at your local garden centre. Follow the general guidelines for buying shrubs when choosing annuals.

Buying equipment and sundries

When buying anything for your garden take time to consider where it has come from, how it has been made and to what extent you will be able to reuse or recycle it, if necessary. Many products are now marked with the mobius loop (three arrows going around in a triangle), which shows that the article can be recycled. The percentage figure in the centre of the loop shows how much is made of recycled materials.

Try to avoid too much packaging or aim for packaging that is recycled, recyclable, reusable or biodegradable. Plastic pots can soon mount up but they are useful for growing on young plants, and places such as schools with gardens may be grateful for them.

Try to buy locally; many items may not be any more expensive and you will have the satisfaction of knowing exactly where your furniture etc. came from. Be especially careful when buying wooden furniture to check that it has come from a renewable source and has not been made from illegally felled rainforest trees.

Planting

The most important consideration when planting anything is to make sure it is positioned in a spot where it will be happy. It is a complete waste of time, effort and money to put a sun-loving plant in deepest shade, however much you may want it to grow there. You must also make sure that the eventual size of the plant and its roots will be suitable for your chosen spot. This is particularly important for trees; they should never be planted too near buildings because of the spread of their roots.

Timing is also important. Autumn and spring are usually the best times to plant out, depending on the plant and the condition of the soil. Spring is best if you have heavy soil that could become waterlogged during the winter, and for less hardy and evergreen plants. All tender annuals must not be planted out until after the last frost. Basic planting rules apply to everything:

- The hole must be large enough to accommodate the roots comfortably.
- The plant should be surrounded by a mixture of compost and soil. You want a reasonably rich mixture to help the plant settle in but not so rich that the roots will not spread out into the soil beyond. If you make the mixture too rich the roots will stay within it and simply grow around in circles. This can be a particular problem in heavy soils that the roots may find hard to penetrate.
- The plant must be fixed gently but firmly into the soil.
- Plenty of water should be given before and after planting; this applies to everything, even drought-tolerant plants.

Planting container-grown shrubs

These can be planted at any time but the soil should not be too wet, too dry or frozen. (See figure 7.3)

1 Water the plant well.
2 Dig a hole to the correct depth and double the width of the pot and loosen the soil at the bottom of the hole.
3 Gently remove the plant from the pot by turning the pot on its side and tapping the sides and bottom. Never pull a plant out of its container by its stem.
4 Loosen some root ends to encourage them to grow outwards.
5 Put the plant in the hole so the soil mark on the stem is fractionally above the level of the top of the hole. This will stop it getting waterlogged.
6 Fill in with a mixture of soil and compost.
7 Firm the soil into place gently using your hands or the ball of your foot.
8 Water well and mulch (see page 111) putting a 5 cm/2 in layer on the ground covered by the spread of the branches as this is a good indicator of the area the roots will cover. Leave a gap immediately around the stem so it will not rot.

Planting container-grown trees

1 Fix a stake so it is on the windward side of the tree as this will give maximum support. The height of the stake above the ground will depend on the tree, but 90 cm/3 ft is usually sufficient unless the tree's stem is very flexible. Use buckle and spacer ties to hold the tree in place and check them regularly to make sure that they do not become too tight as the tree grows.
2 Follow steps 1–8 above for planting container-grown shrubs.
3 If you need to add a stake after you have planted the tree, put it in at an angle so you do not damage the roots.
4 After two years, shake the tree gently and if the roots remain firm you can remove the stake. Always do this at the beginning of the growing season so that the tree can gain strength while the climate is mild.

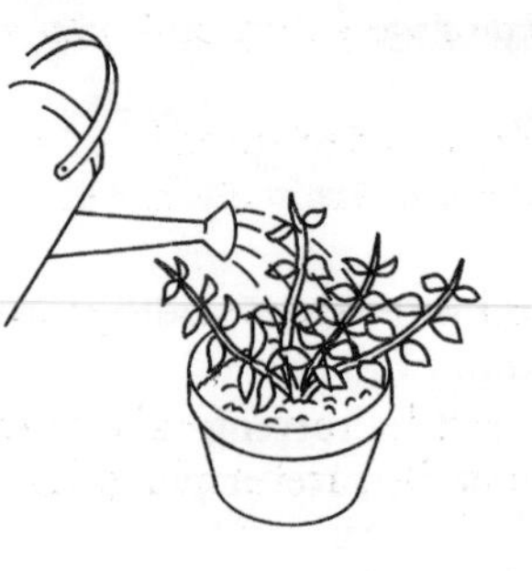

first water the plant, then check the hole is deep enough

remove the plant gently from the pot

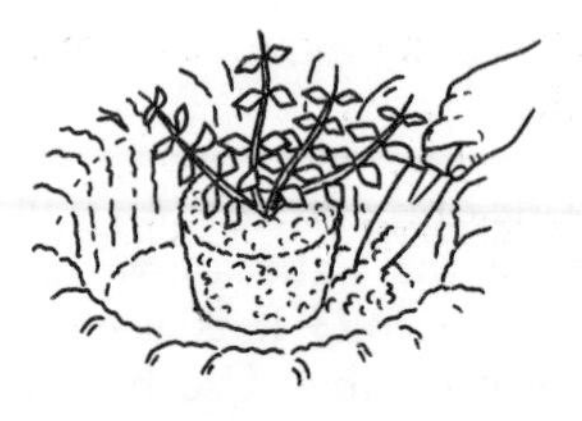

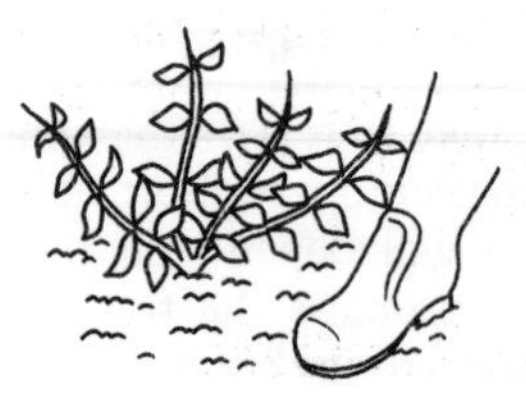

position in the hole, fill gently with soil and compost and finally tread down firmly

figure 7.3 how to plant container-grown shrubs

Planting bare-rooted trees and shrubs

It is vital that the roots should never be allowed to dry out and, with this in mind, all bare-rooted plants should be heeled in or permanently planted as soon as possible. This is best done between late autumn and early spring.

1 Prune any roots that are disproportionately long and remove any damaged ones.
2 Dig a hole wide enough to allow the roots to spread out and down, with the soil mark on the stem fractionally above the surface of the ground.
3 Fix the stake in place, as Step 1 for planting container-grown trees, above.
4 Holding the tree or shrub in place, gently trowel in a mixture of soil and compost around the roots. Be careful not to leave any air pockets.
5 Fill to the surface and gently firm down. Do not press as hard as you would with a container-grown plant as the roots are more vulnerable.
6 Water and mulch as Step 8 for container-grown strubs above.

Planting roses

The planting techniques are the same as for shrubs (see page 107) except as follows.

- Mix plenty of well-rotted manure and bone meal at the base of the hole.
- Position the plant so that the joint where the rootstock starts is 2.5 cm/1 in below the surface of the ground.
- After planting, prune back to two or three buds per stem. This may seem vicious but it will encourage more vigorous growth.

Planting climbers

The soil at the base of walls tends to be dry so position the plants 30–45 cm/12–18 in away. Plant as for shrubs (see page 107). After planting, untie the stems and gently spread them out and train them in the correct directions. Remove all the ties and add new ones, using soft green twine, which will allow for growth.

Clematis should be planted 8 cm/3 in below the level of the soil to encourage strong shoots that will be better able to withstand the potentially fatal problem of clematis wilt.

Planting bulbs

Bulbs need to be planted six months before they flower. The exceptions are tulips, which can be planted any time from late autumn to mid-winter. If you want to leave your bulbs permanently in place they should have twice their own depth of soil above them. You can even plant them deeper, up to 30 cm/ 12 in so they are well out of the way of other plants above. This is hard work though, and if you only want a temporary display from your bulbs, for example, in a container, you do not need to plant them nearly so deeply. Twice their depth is ideal but most will be fine 5 cm/2 in under the surface. If you are planting a lot of bulbs, a bulb planter makes the job much easier as it digs holes exactly the right shape (see page 94).

- Make sure you plant your bulbs the right way up; the pointy part should be facing upwards. When planting corms it may not be obvious which way they should go. If in doubt, lay them on their sides as this will not do as much harm as planting them upside down.
- If your soil is heavy, reduce the planting depth.
- Put sand or grit at the base of the hole so the bulb will not rot.
- Embed the roots firmly in the sand or grit and fill the hole, ensuring no air is trapped.
- For a natural look, scatter the bulbs by hand and plant them where they land.

Planting perennials and annuals

Perennials are usually best planted in spring or autumn and the method is the same as for shrubs (see page 107). Annuals should be planted in late spring to early summer, depending on whether they are hardy or not. Remember that annuals in particular are delicate and should always be lifted by the root ball rather than the stem.

Supports

You will need to provide support for many annuals and perennials and even for some bulbs.

- Bamboo canes and soft twine are good for individual plants.
- Twiggy branches can be pushed into the soil. The plants will grow up through the branches and rest on the twigs, hiding them from view.
- Metal poles covered with plastic can be used to enclose plants and keep them upright. They can be hoop-shaped or will link together to form a network of squares or triangles.

- Posts or canes can be put in at the corners of the bed with plastic netting spread between them. Netting with 5 cm/2 in squares will provide support without being obtrusive.

Any support should be just below the final height of the plant so that it will provide maximum support but will be largely hidden from view once the flower is in bloom.

Mulching

Mulch is a layer of matter that you put on top of the soil around plants. It can be organic matter, such as compost or bark, or inorganic, like plastic or gravel. According to what sort of mulch you use, it has various functions:

- Preventing the growth of weeds or wind erosion of bare soil.
- Keeping the soil warm in winter and cool in summer.
- Reducing evaporation while letting rain through and so conserving water.
- Enriching the soil.
- Making the garden look attractive.

No single mulch will do everything, so use the list below to work out what you need and, if necessary, use a combination.

- Bark has little nutritional value but is attractive, improves the structure of the soil, prevents evaporation and deters slugs and snails. Use composted bark as this will break down better.
- Garden compost is the best mulch but it is unlikely you will be able to make enough for all your needs.
- Farm manure must be well rotted and it can contain weed seeds, but it is nutritional and will improve the soil structure as it breaks down.
- Mushroom compost is excellent but it is alkaline so you cannot use it around lime-intolerant plants.
- Leaf mould is good but it takes a long time to make, does not look attractive and can be acidic.
- Cocoa shells are a by-product of the chocolate industry. They are nutritional but tend to be acidic and are very light, only being stable when wet.
- Grass can lose nitrogen as it decomposes. It does not look attractive and must be spread thinly so it does not form a solid mat.

- Seaweed is a good mulch but is really only practical if you live near the sea. You can leave it to rot down first or wash the salt off and dig it in straight away.
- Straw and hay form a good barrier over the soil and are useful for plants such as strawberries. Composted straw or 'Strulch™' is a better general mulch.
- Grit or pebbles have no nutritional value but reduce evaporation and weeds and deter slugs and snails. They can look attractive if you ensure they do not mix with the soil below.
- Polythene, old newspapers and carpet will all deter weeds but have no nutritional value and look unattractive.

To be effective, the mulch must be at least 5 cm/2 in deep and should be laid down at planting time and thereafter in spring and autumn. The soil should be well prepared beforehand, i.e. weed-free, well nourished and damp. Mulch is usually best applied with a spade, or a trowel around smaller plants. This makes ure that you spread an even layer over the soil and leave a gap immediately around the stems of plants to stop the damp mulch causing them to rot (see Figure 7.4).

figure 7.4 when applying mulch, always leave a gap around the plant stem so it does not get damp and rot

Green manure

This can almost be described as a growing mulch. Usually fast-growing agricultural crops are used, and cut down and dug into the soil before they set seed. Depending which you use, green manure can fix nitrogen in the soil for later use (clover, vetches and winter field beans) or improve soil structure (alfalfa has deep roots). Rye and other grasses will suppress weeds and all will help the soil when they are dug in. It is vital to cut them down before they set seed and dig them into the ground before they get too big and tough. They are especially useful for fallow areas of a vegetable garden or ornamental areas that you haven't yet got around to planting up.

Compost

Making your own compost is an important and incredibly satisfying part of gardening. It is easy, need not take up much space, and will give you wonderful, nutritious organic matter with which to enrich your soil. It is not, or should not be, messy or smelly! In order to create good compost, all you need is the correct balance of ingredients and a warm, dry place for it to decompose (see Figure 7.5). It is no good simply throwing all your green waste onto a heap and hoping for the best. There are a number of compost bins available:

- Wooden or brick-built compost bins with a lid are the most satisfactory as they will keep the warmth in and the damp out.
- Plastic is not so well insulated as wood or brick but is cheaper and can be bought in smaller sizes if necessary.
- Wormeries come complete with the worms needed to make really good compost. They take up little space and produce good compost relatively quickly.
- A huge range of attractive bins disguised to look like beehives etc. are perfect for smaller gardens where the compost area cannot be hidden.
- If you have room it is worth having two compost bins so you can be filling one up while the other is maturing (see Figure 7.6).

It is important to keep a balance between the layers of green matter or household waste, and the layers of straw or twigs or even shredded paper, which will help the air to circulate. Each layer should be no more than 10 cm/4 in thick. You can also add a 2.5-cm/1 in layer of soil every 15–30 cm/6–12 in if you wish, which will bulk it up. Turning your compost will mix the ingredients, introduce air and encourage it to decompose more quickly; with one turn in warm weather it should be ready in three months, six in winter. Compost accelerators should not be necessary if you have a good balance of ingredients. When you turn the compost, you may see little red worms. They are very beneficial and help decomposition. They should appear naturally, but you can also buy them if necessary. Things you can compost include the following.

- All uncooked kitchen waste including tea leaves, coffee grounds and eggshells. Avoid meat as this may encourage rats. Potato peelings may sprout!
- Annual weeds if they have not set seed. Do not compost perennial weeds as they will simply put out roots and start to grow.
- Grass cuttings should be mixed with other matter, otherwise they will form an impenetrable layer that will stop the air circulating.
- Woody or thorny material will decompose slowly but a layer of twigs at the bottom will help air circulation.
- Earthy roots will lower the overall temperature and slow the process down.
- Leaves can be added but leaf mould is usually better made separately as it takes much longer to decompose. Oak and beech leaves are traditionally considered the best, and London plane should be avoided as it takes too long. Construct a heap of 15 cm/6 in leaves to 2.5 cm/1 in soil or put in a black plastic bag. This should be left for one year and used as a mulch the following autumn.
- Unused crops of fruit and vegetables, although this seems rather a waste!
- Shredded paper, ripped up cardboard or straw. You cannot compost any packaging, such as plastic, which is non-biodegradable.

Compost is ready to use when all the separate elements have broken down and it is pleasantly crumbly. Compost should not smell or have a slimy feel, and none of the original ingredients should be identifiable. If it is too dry you can add water or green waste. If it is too wet or smelly add paper, cardboard or straw. Turn or stir to introduce more air and leave uncovered if the weather is dry. Slugs, snails, mice and voles are harmless but watch out for rats, which may be attracted by the warmth. Not composting meat products should reduce any problems. It is unlikely you will be able to make enough compost for all your needs, but whatever you make will greatly enrich your garden.

figure 7.5 cross-section of home-made compost showing a layer of fibrous stems at the bottom, then a layer of kitchen waste, grass and straw, then a thin layer of soil. The general refuse and straw can be repeated to the top

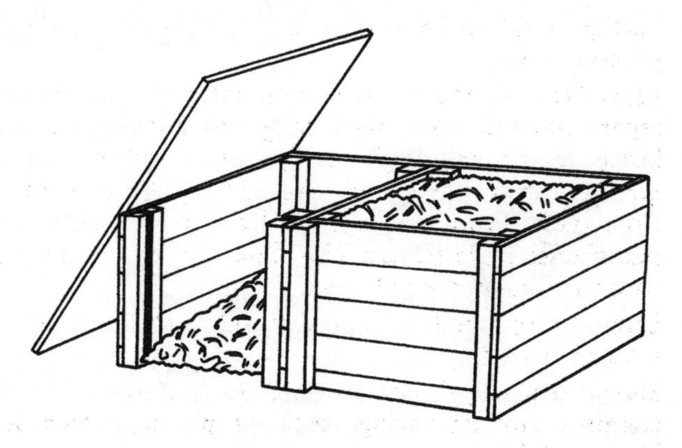

figure 7.6 a double bin with removable front panel allows you to use one batch of compost while the other matures

Feeding

If you mulch the soil with well-rotted manure or garden compost you will have already provided your garden with much of the food it needs. Gardeners require plants to put on an unnaturally spectacular display and also to grow in unnatural proximity to other plants. For plants to develop and thrive in this way, you may have to provide them with more nutrients than they might need if they were growing naturally in the wild. Plants benefit most from food that is supplied during their growing season, i.e. mid-spring to midsummer, but all supplements work best if the soil is damp. There are three main minerals your plants may need:

1 Nitrogen (N) – encourages leaf growth and is particularly useful for grass and leafy vegetables. A deficiency is indicated by weak stems and small leaves.
2 Phosphorous or phosphates (P) – important for most development and necessary for young plants, root vegetables and fruits. A deficiency is indicated by stunted stems, small, purplish leaves and low fruit yield.
3 Potassium or potash (K) – helps the plant produce flowers and fruit and is also necessary for potatoes. A deficiency is indicated by yellow or brown leaves, a low yield of flowers or fruit and a tendency towards disease.

Small amounts of calcium, iron and zinc are also needed but it is rare to have to add these.

In practice, your plants are unlikely to suffer from a serious deficiency of anything. However, if you ask a lot from your plants it can help to feed them, for example, potassium or tomato food will extend the flowering season of annuals. You may be able to establish a good balance simply by mulching, but in a small space and especially in containers a little extra food can help. Whatever you are using, always be careful to follow the instructions as too much of a supplement can be as harmful as too little. The ways to add nutrients are as follows.

- Solid food – granules can be sprinkled around the base of the plant or put into the soil at the time of planting. Slow-release sticks of fertilizer can be stuck in the soil, and animal manure in pellets can be scattered on the surface. Try to avoid contact with the leaves as they can be scorched.
- Liquid food – this is administered via a watering can or hose attachment. Again, avoid too much contact with the leaves.

- Foliar feed – this is taken in via the leaves. As it goes directly into the sap it is useful for sick plants that may not have a strong root system. Spray during still dry evenings to get the maximum benefit.

Always choose organic feeds because these will benefit your plants without harming the environment. Ask for advice when buying food at your local garden centre as many of the staff will have gardens in the area and know what is most suitable. If you have children or pets always check that the product you are using will not harm them.

Watering

More so than food, water is essential for your plants' survival. The amount varies enormously, but all plants need some water. It is a common mistake to think that all plants need vast amounts of water; once they are established many plants need little extra water, which is good news in these days of climate change and increasing hose pipe bans. It is worth identifying which groups of plants do need extra water.

- Trees and shrubs will need regular water for their first two years while they settle in. Most perennials will need regular supplies for their first year and annuals and vegetables throughout their lives. Remember that this means *sufficient* water – you do not need to swamp your plants. In fact, if you keep them slightly short of water you will encourage them to be tougher and to put out a more extensive root system.
- Plants within 60 cm/2 ft of a wall will need regular watering throughout their lives as the wall will absorb water.
- Containers, especially if terracotta, do not store water well and will need watering most days in hot weather. Hanging baskets may need watering twice a day, early in the morning and again in the evening.

The exact amounts of water that you should give are not specified here as there are too many variables, including your soil, the density of your planting and the general climate. Remember that wind can dry out plants as fast, if not faster, than sunshine.

It is important to water plants before they wilt; a good test is to feel how damp the soil is 5 cm/2 in below the surface. If it is dry you need to water. It is best to water in the evening, but you can water during the day if necessary as long as you avoid watering in direct sunshine. Never aim a strong hose jet directly at the plant as you can easily damage the leaves and wash soil away from around the roots.

It is better to water shrubs and trees thoroughly once a week rather than giving them a little every day. Once they are established, perennials prefer this too. Small amounts of water encourage little surface roots that are more vulnerable than deep-set ones. There are a number of ways of watering your garden, some more efficient than others:

- **Watering cans** are in many ways the best way to water as they force you to look at each plant as you water it. This means that you will give the plant exactly the amount it needs and also that you will notice if there are any problems, such as aphids or deadheading, that need to be dealt with.
- **Hoses** are fine as long as a ban is not in operation and you water in the evening when little will be lost through evaporation. Always spray the water gently at the base of the plant. Do not leave the hose running into a bed; you will probably end up swamping it.
- **Sprinklers** may seem like a good idea, but they are wasteful because much of the water is lost through evaporation and the rest lands on the leaves and not at the base where it is really needed. As explained in Chapter 05 (page 80), watering lawns is not particularly beneficial.
- **Irrigation systems** can be very efficient and are worth considering if you have a large garden or are away frequently or you just don't like the idea of having to water regularly. They usually work on a drip system, where spurs come off the main pipe and drip water onto the roots, or by a perforated pipe or leaky hose system that has small holes which leak water onto the plant. These systems are good as they aim the water directly at the base of the plant and you can regulate the amounts used.
- **Water butts** are an excellent way of collecting water and can be positioned so the run-off from the gutters flows in to them. If using a wooden butt, ensure it is treated and fully waterproof. Always cover the butt with a lid to prevent algae growing and small animals (and children) falling in. Purpose-built water butts are available with a pipe through the lid to allow water in and a tap further down the side to let it out.

- **Recycled grey water** is fine for ornamental plants as long as you use ecological soaps and washing powders, and let the water cool down first!
- **Water-retaining gels or crystals** are tiny granules that can hold 100 times their size in water. They also create spaces within the soil and prevent it becoming compacted. These are especially useful in containers where they will also keep the soil cool in hot weather by holding water in it.

A final way to conserve water is to create shallow depressions around the base of larger plants, which can be used to prevent water running off and being wasted. This is described in the 'Drought conditions' section on page 21.

In hot summers, much is made of how wasteful we are with water. It is important to remember that while humans use (and waste) a huge amount of water, gardeners who water responsibly do not actually use that much. Do not overwater your plants but, equally, do not starve them.

Dealing with pests, diseases and weeds

However careful you are, at some time your plants will suffer at the hands (or roots) of pests, diseases or weeds. Pests are animals or insects that harm plants by eating them or living on them. Diseases are caused by fungus, viruses or bacteria. Weeds are plants growing where they are not wanted, usually at the expense of more choice specimens. Any plant's resistance to pests and diseases may be reduced by disorders that are caused by poor growing conditions. Always ensure that your plants are in the right situation, growing in suitable soil and have the correct amount of water. If you do this they will be in good condition and ready to fight off most problems.

From the outset, it is worth facing up to the fact that your garden will never be perfect. Most plant problems in the garden result in disfigurement rather than permanent damage, and if you try and eliminate all pests and diseases you will turn your garden into a war zone and never be able to relax in it. You need to adopt a slightly firmer approach regarding fruit and vegetables as you do not want to lose your entire crop, but even here it is better if you are prepared to compromise a little. You should avoid using chemical products because they will upset the natural balance of your garden. Any change may not be immediately apparent and may not even do any great harm but the more we discover about the use of chemicals the more we realize how damaging their effect is on the environment. Many chemicals that were thought to be safe 30 years ago have now been withdrawn, and although this means that chemicals in use now tend to be less harmful you can never be sure of their impact. Derris, which had been manufactured from plants for almost 100 years and had organic approval, has now been banned, showing how uncertain this whole area is. Also some pests have to be lived with rather than eradicated. If your garden has slugs it will continue to have slugs to some extent regardless of how many slug pellets you put down. You may also destroy useful predators at the same time as trying to wipe out the slugs (some pellets can be harmful to hedgehogs and birds who eat slugs). The best solution is to protect vulnerable plants and not worry too much otherwise.

As with so much in gardening, prevention rather than cure is the ideal to aim for. If you buy healthy plants, choosing resistant strains where possible, and provide suitable conditions for them, they should be able to withstand the onslaught of any pests and diseases. It also helps if you keep your garden reasonably clean and tidy. You do not want it to be so clinical that you drive all the wildlife away, but it is worth clearing away heaps of weeds and leaves rather than letting them rot near other plants where they may cause disease. It also helps if you deal with any problems as soon as they appear. Keeping on top of pests and diseases may sound like an endless vigil, but don't worry too much – deal with any serious problems if and when they arise and let everything else take care of itself; it can.

Pests

Organic methods for dealing with problems include:

- ensuring your plants are as healthy and happy as possible, as described above
- trying to get nature on your side by encouraging helpful predators
- using companion planting to deter pests
- deploying naturally-derived products to deal with any problems that do occur.

Companion planting is a useful method of pest control as one plant provides protection for another, for example, garlic planted with roses will deter aphids. It is particularly useful for vegetables and is covered in detail in Chapter 09 (see page 162). Crop rotation is most common in kitchen gardens but it is also worth gently practising it in an ornamental garden. Try to avoid planting the same annuals or biennials in the same place year after year and you will prevent a build-up of bacteria and ensure that the soil does not develop an imbalance.

Various organically-approved products are available that are made from plant or mineral extracts. Their effects are fairly short lived so you may need to re-treat the plants at regular intervals.

- Pyrethrum is made from the pyrethrum plant and is used to control insects. Unfortunately it is harmful to all insects so you should only use it in the evening when beneficial insects, such as bees and ladybirds, are no longer flying around.
- Soft soap products are available that are effective against aphids but do not harm ladybirds or other insects.
- Nematodes are worms that can destroy certain pests.

Common pests and how to deal with them

Slugs and snails

These are probably at the top of every gardener's hit list. Slugs live in soil and snails in brickwork, so depending on your garden you may be unlucky and have both. There are almost as many solutions as there are gardeners, so test a few and see which works best for you. Putting them in salt water or offering them beer (in which they drown) are popular solutions but you are left with a horrible mass of squishy corpses. Organic slug pellets made from ferric phosphate are reasonably successful and the nematode *Phasmarhabditis hermaphrodita* works well but both need to be regularly re-applied. A good method, especially in a small garden, is to provide protection for vulnerable or young plants. Sharp mulch or gravel will create a slug- and snail-proof barrier. Salt, soot, eggshells and orange peel will do the same, but look as unattractive as a chewed plant. Sequestered seaweed will feed the soil and deter them. Copper tape can be put around pots. These barriers need to be about 2.5 cm/1 in wide and will last until the soil is disturbed. With all of them it is vital that no leaves overhang and act as edible bridges. The most vulnerable plants are clematis, lupins, hostas, delphiniums, marigolds, stocks, tobacco plants, tulips, almost anything when it is young, and many vegetables. Spiky or hairy plants, those with leathery leaves and most herbs are safe.

Aphids

Aphids suck the sap of plants and can distort growth and increase the risk of disease and mould. They include green, brown and black fly. Roses, honeysuckle, nasturtiums, potatoes, carrots and lettuce are at most risk. Birds, lacewings and ladybirds will all help but they are unlikely to be able to solve the problem for you as aphids breed so fast. In a small garden, you can remove aphids by hand. A strong jet of water will dislodge them, as will a weak soap solution, but these methods cannot be used on young plants. A weak solution of seaweed spray will get rid of the aphids and benefit the plant. Garlic will act as a deterrent if grown alongside vulnerable plants. Simply push a clove into the ground and let it grow up. The leaves are unobtrusive and the smell of the garlic will not be transferred to the other plants. Nematodes can also be used.

Ants

These can weaken roots with their nests and they also 'farm' aphids as they eat the honeydew that aphids excrete. The best way to destroy the nests is to pour boiling water into them.

Caterpillars

Caterpillars eat leaves and flowers but they provide valuable food for birds and do eventually turn into beautiful butterflies. Nematodes are available, but remember that you will be killing the butterfly that would emerge from the catepillar. An alternative, if slightly antisocial solution is to throw the caterpillars into your neighbour's garden and hope that they come back as butterflies! Basil, borage, hyssop, rosemary, sage and thyme will deter the cabbage white caterpillar.

Vine weevils

These cause particular problems in containers. The adults eat leaves and lay their eggs in the soil and the grubs then eat the plant's roots. Vines, camellias and heucheras are also at risk. Between spring and autumn the adults can be killed by applying nematodes (*Heterorhabditis megadis* or *Steinemana carpocapsoe*) or you can put barrier glue around the container.

Shield bugs

These eat a variety of soft fruits and vegetables and increase the risk of disease on all plants. The brown type is relatively harmless but the bright green ones can do great harm. They are easy to spot and can be picked off and killed.

Red lily beetle

This is a conspicuous bright red beetle that does great damage to lilies. Pick off and kill any you see.

Moles

Moles can ruin lawns but spurge or rue planted around the edge will deter them. There are innumerable other deterrents ranging from the smell of garlic or moth balls to the sound of a radio or the vibration of a toy windmill or flag. Any of these should be placed at the entrance to the tunnel and will drive the mole away. Traps are available but seem unnecessarily cruel for such appealing animals.

Rabbits

Rabbits can be a big problem as they will eat all young plants and many older ones. You can put wire collars around young plants or fence off the whole area but the netting needs to be 1 m/3 ft tall with at least one quarter below ground. Alternatively, get a dog!

As our climate changes, many pests are spreading to new areas. If you encounter something you do not recognize, take a sample to be identified so you can deal with it. Remember that not all creatures that appear in the garden are a nuisance. It is well known that ladybirds eat aphids, but so do hoverflies and lacewings. Although birds are pests regarding fruit, they have their uses as many eat slugs and snails. Frogs, toads and shrews are also invaluable helpers, as are hedgehogs.

Common diseases

As always, prevention is better than cure. Ensure your plants are strong and healthy, grown in the correct soil and have the correct amount of water. Allowing air to circulate will reduce the risk of fungal growth, so do not put your plants too close together, and prune trees and shrubs so their centres are not congested. Always disinfect tools after dealing with a diseased plant, and destroy any diseased leaves or stems rather than adding them to your compost. It is increasingly possible to buy disease-resistant varieties and these are well worth growing.

Black spot

This is common on roses and, although unsightly, it does little harm. You can remove the affected leaves.

Blight

Blight can be a problem for tomatoes and potatoes. The leaves turn brown and die and the fruits then become discoloured and rot. Ensure air can circulate around the plant and avoid overhead watering.

Botrytis (grey mould)

This appears as fluffy grey mould on faded flowers and leaves. You should cut away any diseased parts, increase the air circulation, and reduce the moisture within the plant.

Canker

Canker causes wrinkled bark and stems. Cut away affected parts. Bad drainage may be a cause.

Honey fungus

This is probably the most serious problem you will encounter. Black strands grow up the stems and eventually the plant dies. You must dig up the plant and all its roots and destroy them. You should leave the soil for two years before planting another shrub and then choose a resistant variety such as yew, beech, clematis, ivy or honeysuckle. During the two-year gap you can grow annuals.

Leaf curl

This causes the leaves to drop early. Remove diseased stems and spray new growth with a weak seaweed solution.

Powdery mildew

This is caused by dryness and appears as white powder on the leaves and stems. Water well and mulch.

Rust

Rust appears as small brown or orange patches on the leaves. Remove the affected leaves, improve the air circulation, and spray the plant with a weak seaweed solution.

Scab

Scab especially attacks apples, pears and pyracantha and causes blemishes on the fruit. Remove infected fruit; you can eat it but do not store it. Remove infected leaves and prune to improve ventilation.

Weeds

Most weeds do not look particularly attractive and they take up space, nutrients and water that could be better used by the plants you actually want to grow. Weeds are a particular threat to young plants because they are native to the area, have chosen a spot perfect for their needs, and will probably be stronger and grow faster than many of the specimens you have planted yourself. Clearing an area of invasive weeds can be hard work and in some cases disheartening as weeds have a tendency to reappear with alarming speed. Weeds can be divided into two groups that need slightly different treatments – annual and perennial weeds.

Annual weeds

Annial weeds complete their life cycle within a year and the vital thing is to prevent them from setting seed. An old saying goes that, 'One weed's seeds are seven years' weeding'. That is, if you allow annual weeds to seed you will be dealing with the consequences for seven years. However, annual weeds are not totally bad. Apart from anything else they indicate that the soil is fertile. Most are reasonably easy to pull up, they will enrich the compost heap (only add them before they set seed otherwise they will grow in the compost), and if you do not want to dig them up you can hoe them as they appear, which will deal with the problem on a temporary level and weaken the weeds in the long run.

Perennial weeds

Perennial weeds can be more serious problem, particularly some of the invasive ones that will take over your garden if given half a chance. Some spread by seed but most have large and efficient root systems – if you leave 1 cm/½ in of some roots in the soil the plant will quickly re-grow. If you regularly remove the surface growth, you will weaken the plant and reduce the problem but you are unlikely to kill it totally. Perennial plants that you dig up should not be put on the compost as they will grow there. The six worst perennial weeds are bindweed, ground elder, couch grass, dock, horsetail and Japanese knotweed.

Methods of weed control

Depending on your strength, patience and inclination there are various ways of dealing with weeds. If you are preparing a site from scratch, it may be tempting to wipe out the weeds using chemicals but many will remain in the soil and may do harm in the long run.

Hand pulling seems laborious, but it is the best method for weeds found growing in among flowerbeds. It is better to do a small area really thoroughly than a large area roughly. Make sure you remove the whole plant and clear it all away immediately.

Hoeing is a relatively easy method of weeding and is particularly useful in kitchen gardens where the plants are growing in straight lines. While hoeing will not get rid of perennial weeds, it should reduce the annual ones and will keep your problem under control quite easily. Always make sure the blade is sharp, the soil dry and that you do not put the hoe blade too far below the surface. You must also be careful that you do not hoe neighbouring plants. If the soil is damp, rake up the weeds so they are not tempted to take root again.

Digging is the best approach if you have an area infested with weeds. First, dig up any plants you want to save and wash them under a tap to ensure no weed roots remain, dividing the plant if necessary. Second, dig over the area thoroughly with a fork and remove all the roots. Turning the soil will unearth some annual weeds but they will be easy to remove as they appear.

Another alternative for a large area is to grow a crop that will suppress weeds. Rye grass should be left for two years, kept short, and this will smother most weeds. You can then dig in the grass and plant up the bed. Potatoes can also be grown and will drive out most weeds within a year. The roots of *Tagetes minuta*, a type of marigold, are useful as they put out a substance that deters couch grass and ground elder.

Ground-cover plants can be used to suppress weeds but you will need to weed for the first couple of years while the plants become established, and then mulch regularly. Be careful that they do not grow too rampantly and take over – Japanese knotweed began life as a garden plant.

Mulching will suppress most weeds providing it is at least 5 cm/ 2 in deep. Solid covering, such as black plastic, newspapers or old carpeting weighed down, will suppress any growth but it does not look attractive and it may take two to three seasons to destroy all perennials completely. If you adopt this method it is possible to disguise the covering by putting a layer of bark on top.

Flame guns may seem a drastic and dangerous approach but can be very successful. The flames burn all the surface weeds and are particularly useful for destroying annuals and their seeds. The downside is that you may have to treat the area several times in one season. Take care not to destroy or damage surrounding plants or resident wildlife.

Of course, some weeds are perfectly acceptable and can be encouraged. Unless you want an immaculate lawn with stripes, daisies look very attractive in among the grass, and cow parsley along hedges and under trees looks beautiful. Even nettles have their uses as they encourage butterflies and can be used for soup! There is a fine and wavy dividing line between wild flowers and weeds.

Pruning

Many plants in a garden need pruning – sometimes for their own well-being but more often to encourage them to perform in a certain way. Plants frequently need their size or shape restricted and are also often required to produce an unnatural amount of flowers or fruit. Moreover, we usually want the flowers and fruit at a certain height, for example, many climbers will only produce flowers at their very top if left to themselves whereas judicious pruning can encourage them to flower at lower levels, which we can appreciate in the garden. The whole subject may seem overwhelming, but there are various ground rules that apply to most plants.

Pruning is the cutting away of parts of a woody plant, i.e. trees or shrub, but it also extends to deadheading flowering plants. The removal of the foliage of some perennials in autumn is called 'cutting down' rather than 'pruning'.

Pruning is carried out with three main aims:

1 To improve the health or condition of the plant. Dead, diseased or damaged stems should be removed as soon as possible. Branches that grow inwards across the centre of the plant should be removed to increase ventilation and reduce the risk of disease.

2 To improve the size and shape of the plant. Topiary, the art of shaping plants, is really a type of intensive pruning. Light pruning, i.e. trimming the tips of the plant, encourages the plant to bush out, creating a smaller but denser plant. Hard pruning involves the removal of whole branches, which ultimately creates a larger but more open plant.
3 To encourage the plant to produce more flowers or fruit where you want them. Cutting off spent flowers before the plant has a chance to produce seeds will often encourage it to produce more flowers. Cutting off older stems can encourage the production of more flowers or fruit. Plants with attractive winter stems, such as dogwood (*Cornus*), can be encouraged to produce new brighter stems if the old ones are cut back.

How to prune

Pruning should always be done with a sharp pair of secateurs, knife or saw depending on the size of branch you need to cut (see Figure 7.7).

- Never leave a jagged edge, and avoid ripping any bark away as this could cause disease.
- It is important to cut back to a healthy bud or joint, even if this means you have to cut off more than you really want to. The cut stem will push all its energy into the reduced length so it is important that the new growing point (i.e. the bud) can cope with this.
- Check the remaining bud is facing the correct way as it will form the new stem that the plant will grow out from. It is usually better to cut back to an outward facing bud as this will open up the plant by encouraging the plant to grow outwards.
- Make the cut at an angle so the water will drain away rather than down into the bud or joint.

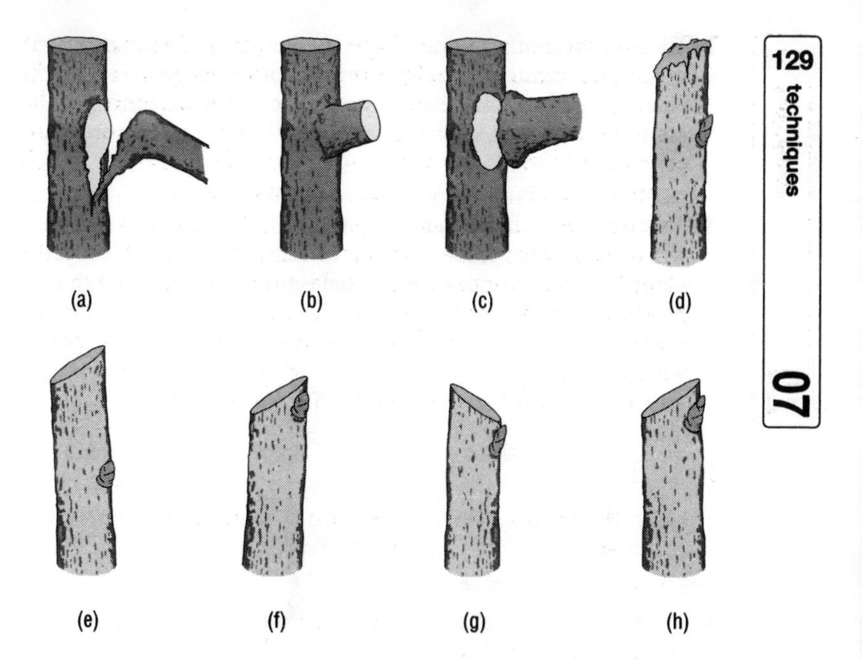

(a) this shows a branch torn away, leaving a jagged edge that could become diseased
(b) this cut leaves too much stem which may die back and cause disease
(c) here the branch has been cut back too close to the main stem
(d) the cut above the bud has been left ragged
(e) the cut is too high above the bud
(f) the cut is too close to the bud
(g) the cut slopes the wrong way
(h) this is the correct cut, cleanly sliced, just above the bed and facing away from it

figure 7.7 incorrect and correct methods of pruning

Large branches should always be cut in sections to avoid damaging the plant (see Figure 7.8):

1 First make a cut upwards into the branch 15 cm/6 in along from where you want to remove the branch. This will ensure that the branch does not pull away and strip the bark.
2 Cut the branch off downwards on the outer side of the first cut, that is, furthest from the trunk or main stem.
3 Once the bulk of the unwanted branch has been removed you can make a neat cut in the final position.

4 When cutting off a branch from the main stem, be careful not to cut into the collar, where the branch meets the main stem. This is usually easy to see as the branch widens out where it joins the stem. Cut at an angle to allow the water to run away harmlessly.
5 Painting large cuts with special substances to prevent disease used to be recommended, but on the whole this is now regarded as unnecessary. After pruning be sure to feed and water the plant as necessary to help it recover from the shock.

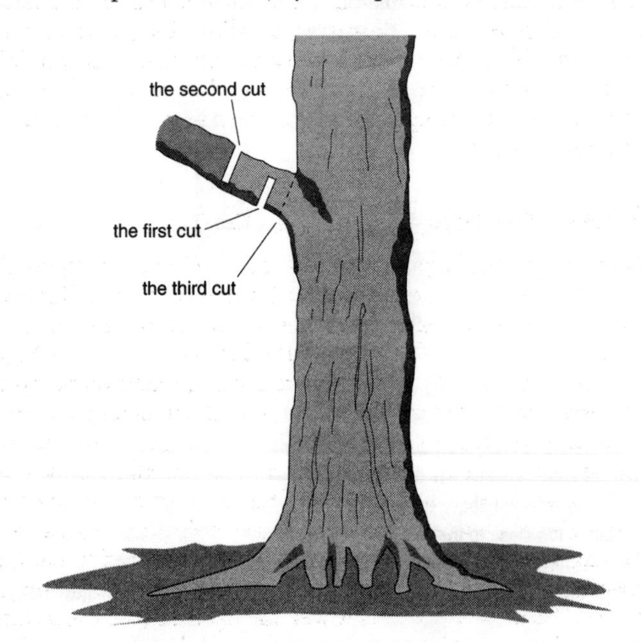

figure 7.8 when removing a large branch, make an undercut first, then cut away the bulk of the branch. This leaves a manageable length of stem that can be cut off at the correct point just beyond the collar where the branch meets the main stem

It is important to be able to distinguish between old and new wood. New growth is usually green and pliable. Old but living wood is normally brown or grey but will be green or white beneath the bark. Cuts made as far back as either of these should readily re-grow. Many plants, such as lavender and conifers, develop a woody base that is brown when cut into. Branches cut back as far as this are unlikely to re-grow and will simply die, possibly killing the entire plant.

The main questions with pruning are when to do it and how much to cut off. Most plants should be given three or four years to establish themselves before you start to prune too much. Generally, it is better to cut too little rather than too much. You are extremely unlikely to harm a plant by under pruning and you can always make more severe cuts next time. If you do remove a flowering stem, the worst that may happen is that you will lose a year's flowers or fruit while the plant re-establishes itself.

As far as timing is concerned, a general but useful rule is that you should prune after flowering to allow the plant as much time as possible to be ready for the next flowering season. With plants that flower late in the summer, this pruning is usually delayed until the spring so that the new growth is not at risk from frost damage.

Winter- or spring-flowering shrubs

Winter- or spring-flowering shrubs mostly flower on stems that have grown over the previous year. Immediately after flowering some of these stems should be removed to allow new shoots to grow up and to be ready to flower the following year (see Figure 7.9). The exact timing of the pruning will depend on when the plant finishes flowering. Dead, diseased or damaged stems should also be removed. Many of these shrubs do not need much pruning, but if you remove some of the old stems it will give the new shoots room to grow. One word of warning: do not cut into the old wood of lavender as it will not re-grow. Start trimming lavender in the first year so you never need to cut back too much. Some of the most common shrubs in this group are: *Berberis*, *Chaenomeles* (Flowering quince), *Cotoneaster*, *Cytisus* (Broom), *Deutzia*, *Forsythia*, *Helianthemum* (Rock rose), *Hydrangea anomala* (Climbing hydrangea), *Jasminium nudiflorum* (Winter jasmine), *Kerria*, *Kolwitzia*, *Lavandula* (Lavender), *Magnolia*, *Passiflora* (Passion flower), *Philadelphus* (Mock orange), *Rhododendron* and *Azalea*, *Ribes sanguineum* (Flowering currant), *Rosmarinus* (Rosemary), *Santolina* (Cotton lavender), *Stachyurus praecox*, *Syringa* (Lilac), *Viburnum* x *bodnantense*, *Weigela*.

figure 7.9 pruning spring-flowering shrubs. In summer, after flowering, cut back some of the stems that have flowered to a strong bud or shoot

Summer-flowering shrubs

Summer-flowering shrubs flower mostly on the current year's growth and should be pruned in the early spring to establish plenty of new stems (see Figure 7.10). If you want to restrict new growth, carry out most of the pruning at the end of the summer so the plant does not store so much energy. Pruning in spring will result in lots of new growth from the energy stored at the end of the previous year. In effect, you are still pruning after flowering but have waited until the danger of frost has passed. These plants usually benefit from hard pruning. Cut back the previous year's growth to a healthy bud, which will then form the new flowering stem. Also cut out any dead, diseased or damaged wood and any stems that are growing where you do not want them. If the plant is liable to be damaged by strong winds during winter, you can part prune it in autumn and finish in the spring. The exceptions to this are hydrangeas, which should have their faded flower heads left in place throughout winter. The most common shrubs in this group are: *Akebia, Buddleja davidii, Campsis* (Trumpet vine), *Caryopteris, Ceanothus, Fuchsia, Hibiscus syriacus, Hydrangea, Lavatera* (Mallow), *Lonicera* (Honeysuckle), *Parthenocissus* (Virginia creeper), *Plumbago, Polygonum, Solanum crispum, S. jasminoides, Tamarix* (Tamarisk), *Thunbergia.*

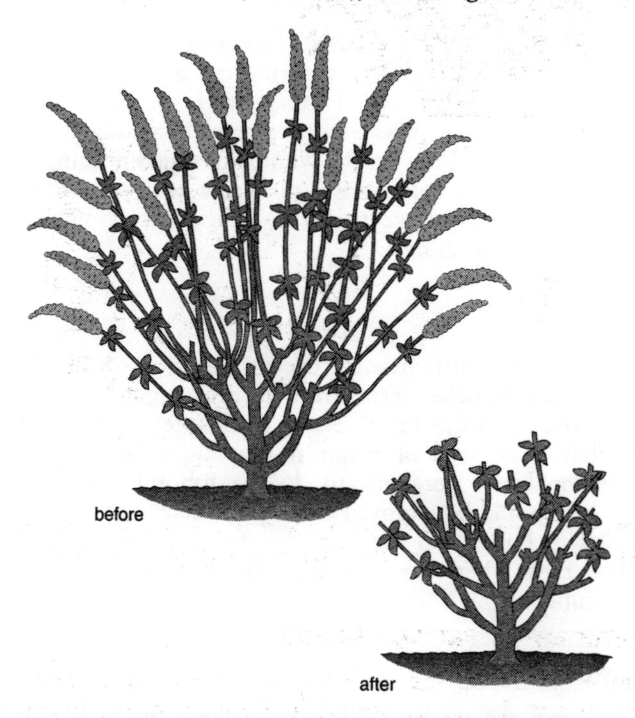

figure 7.10 pruning summer-flowering shrubs. These should be cut back in early to mid-spring. They flower on new growth and should be cut back more severly than spring-flowering shrubs. Cut back all the previous year's growth to within a couple of buds. A permanent woody framework will develop at the base of the plant

Broad-leaved evergreen shrubs

Broad-leaved evergreen shrubs should be pruned in late spring after any danger of frost, or after flowering for spring-flowering species. All dead, diseased and damaged stems should be removed and any branches you want to shorten should be cut back to a suitably facing bud. Extensive pruning should not be necessary. Examples are: *Acuba*, *Camellia*, *Choisya* (Mexican orange blossom), *Elaeagnus*, *Euonymus* (Spindle), *Ilex* (Holly), *Laurus nobilis* (Bay), *Mahonia*, *Osmanthus*, *Sarcococca* (Christmas box).

Conifers

These should be pruned in late summer or early autumn. This is because they bleed sap if cut during the growing season, i.e. spring. In this case the risk of damage to new shoots from frost is less serious than sap loss. Dead, diseased and damaged wood should be removed but on the whole not much pruning should be necessary. Most conifers will not grow new stems if you cut back into old wood; yew (*Taxus*) is the exception and will tolerate harder pruning.

Trees

Most trees need little pruning except to remove dead, diseased or damaged branches. Fruit trees do need regular pruning but this is covered in the 'Fruit' section in Chapter 09. If you have a tree that is in need of major re-shaping, it is better to ask professional tree surgeons to do the job for you. Crossing branches should be removed to keep the centre of the tree well ventilated, but if you keep an eye out you should be able to remove these when they are still small. The timing is the same as for shrubs.

Climbers

Apart from the special cases listed below, the basic rules for pruning shrubs can be applied to climbers. Most climbers benefit from a yearly pruning to keep them in check rather than a drastic cut back every few years. After pruning, ensure any new stems are trained to grow in the direction you want while they are still young and pliable.

Clematis

Pruning clematis is often regarded as a difficult task, but it is in fact perfectly simple as all the plants fall into one of three categories determined by the flowering time. Even if you identify the plant wrongly and cut off too much you are unlikely to do any lasting damage and the plant will probably recover the following year. With all clematis, aim to control the size and ensure the plant flowers all the way down. If left to themselves most clematis will only flower at the top, leaving you with a view of dry, broken stems.

1 Spring-flowering clematis have small flowers that appear in mid- to late spring. You should prune after flowering, but only if you need to reduce the size of the plant as this will not increase the number of flowers. If necessary you can cut the plant right back to 30 cm/1 ft but you must then wait three years for the plant to recover. Examples are: C. *alpina*, C. *armandii*, C. *cirrhosa*, C. *macropetala*, C. *montana*.
2 Summer-flowering clematis have large flowers that appear in early summer on the previous season's shoots. They can also flower later in the season on new growth. You should prune in early spring but do not cut off too much as each bud represents a flower. If the plant gets too big you can either cut it back as for spring-flowering varieties (this will lose the first flush of flowers but the second should do well) or cut one-third of the stems down in spring, one-third down after flowering and the final third the following spring. Examples are: C. 'Barbara Jackman', C. 'Lasurstern', C. 'Lord Neville', C. 'Marie Boisselot', C. 'Mrs N Thompson', C. 'Nelly Moser', C. 'Niobe', C. 'The President', C. 'Richard Pennell', C. 'Vyvyan Pennell'.
3 Late summer to early autumn-flowering clematis have large or medium-size flowers on the current season's growth. After a couple of years, once the plant is established, it should be pruned every year in late winter or early spring. Cut back to a pair of buds 20–30 cm/8–12 in above ground. This will ensure you get leaves and flowers all the way up and down the stems. Example are: C. 'Comtesse de Bouchard', C. 'Ernest Markham', C. 'Gipsy Queen', C. 'Hagley Hibrid', C. 'Jackmanii', C. 'Perle d'Azur', C. *tangutica,* C. 'Ville de Lyon', C. *viticella.*

Wisteria

Wisteria may not flower for the first seven years. Once they are established it is important to prune them twice a year to get the maximum number of flowers. In midsummer, after flowering, all new growth should be cut back to 15 cm/6 in. You can cut the plant back more than once during the summer if it is putting on a lot of growth. In mid-winter, prune again, cutting back all new growth to two or three buds.

Vines (*Vitis*)

Vines should be pruned in early to mid-winter to prevent sap leaking out. Once the framework is established, usually after two or three years, you should shorten all the side shoots to within two or three buds. The main stems will become gnarled and knobbly and look attractive in winter when the plant loses its leaves.

Roses

Unless you are aiming to produce show blooms, the pruning of roses is not that complicated. Tests carried out by the Royal National Rose Society showed that many roses actually produced a greater quantity of blooms when randomly cut back with electrical hedge cutters! As with many other shrubs, if you cut off too much you are unlikely to do any lasting damage.

- Single-flowering shrub roses only need light pruning. After flowering the stems can be reduced by one-third if the plant is becoming too large, and every three years some old stems can be removed at the base to open up the plant. Any dead, diseased or damaged stems should also be removed after flowering.
- Repeat-flowering shrub roses should be regularly deadheaded to encourage more blooms (see below, page 138). They should be pruned in early spring, but if they are liable to be damaged or stressed by strong winter winds you can part prune them in the autumn so they do not blow about too much. These roses mostly flower on new growth so you can cut them back quite hard, always cutting back to a bud facing the direction you want the new stem to take.
- Climbing roses should be pruned between mid-autumn and early spring. Stem growth over three years old tends to be less productive and should be cut down to a bud, which will then grow into a new, flower-bearing stem. Always ensure about six main stems remain. Prune shoots that have flowered by two-thirds their length back to a bud or shoot. Repeat-flowering climbers should be deadheaded regularly throughout their flowering season.
- Rambler roses should be pruned in mid- to late summer after flowering. If you wish to reduce the size, cut a quarter to a third of the stems out at the base. If necessary you can also cut the side shoots back but this will not improve flowering as ramblers flower on old wood.

Hedges

The most important thing with hedges over 1 m/3 ft high is to cut them at an angle so that the leaves grow all the way down. The top can be flat, curved or pointed (see Figure 7.11). When planting a hedge, trim it gently and regularly as it grows up, rather than leaving it until it reaches the required height – this will encourage even growth for the whole height of the hedge.

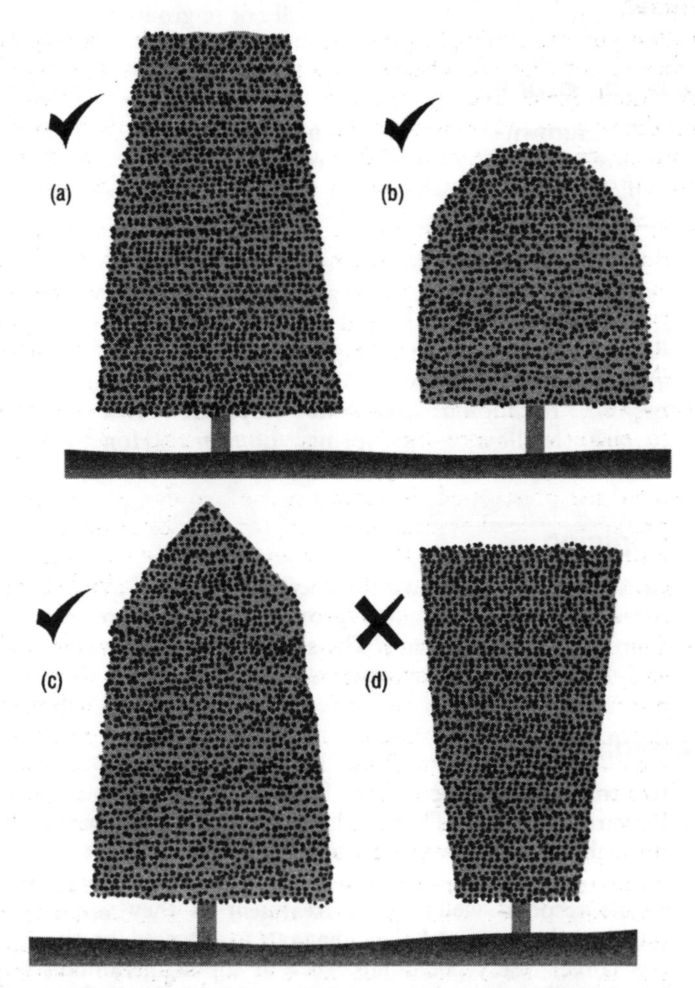

figure 7.11 shapes (a) to (c) are suitable for most types of hedges as light and air can reach all parts. In (d) an area of shadow is created at the base of the plant and stems here will not flourish

When trimming a hedge by hand, always keep the blades parallel to the hedge to ensure the surface is flat. Electric trimmers can be useful for long hedges, but do not use them on large-leaved plants as they tend to rip the leaves rather than cutting them neatly. Formally-shaped hedges usually need to be trimmed twice a year – winter and midsummer for deciduous and late spring and late summer for evergreens. It is particularly important to cut coniferous hedges regularly because if you leave it until you need to cut back into old wood it will not re-grow.

Drastic pruning

Some overgrown shrubs can be renovated by very hard pruning, but there is always an element of risk involved. If for any reason the plant is irreplaceable, treat it gently and carry out the operation over several seasons.

Deciduous plants should be renovated after flowering and evergreens in mid-spring. Cut back one-third to half of the old stems to about 30 cm/1 ft and repeat the following year. The following plants will usually respond to this treatment: *Buddleja davidii* – in spring, *Buxus* (Box), *Choisya* (Mexican orange blossom), *Escallonia*, *Euonymus* (Spindle), *Ilex* (Holly), *Lavatera* (Mallow) – in spring, *Lonicera* (Honeysuckle), *Santolina* (Cotton lavender), *Taxus* (Yew) and *Viburnum*.

Coppicing

This is useful for plants with attractive stems such as dogwood (*Cornus*). It promotes new growth that is more brightly coloured than the old stems. The stems should be cut back to a bud 5–8 cm/2–3 in above the ground in early spring.

Deadheading

This involves removing dead or faded flowers to encourage the production of more. The flower head should be removed by cutting down to the next bud or joint. Remove as little of the stem as necessary, unless you actually want to shorten it. Annuals respond well to this treatment as they will go on producing flowers until they manage to set seed or the first frosts come. Many perennials, such as lupins, geraniums and valerian, will also produce more flowers if deadheaded.

You should not deadhead plants, such as honesty which have attractive seeds, roses which produce hips, or hydrangeas, as their flower heads act as protection for the stems during winter.

It is worth deadheading bulbs, such as tulips and daffodils (*Narcissus*), once the flowers fade. This will not produce more blooms but will allow the plants to concentrate on storing energy for the following year. Bulbs with attractive heads, such as alliums, can be left. Do not cut back the leaves of bulbs, however untidy they may look, as it is through them that the plant gathers energy.

Propagation

It is perfectly possible to buy all the plants for your garden but it can be rewarding to grow some of them yourself. There is a variety of reasons for doing this:

- It is by far the cheapest way of stocking your garden.
- If you choose the right plants and methods it is straightforward and need not take up much space.
- You can grow exactly the plants you want and not what the garden centre dictates. All nurseries, garden centres and mail-order companies have a much wider range of seeds than plants.
- Once you get started it is extremely satisfying and many people find propagation completely addictive!

If you become keen on propagation, there is a wealth of specialist information available (see 'Taking it further', page 194). Here we simply describe the main types of propagation and show you how to get started with the easiest methods to see if you enjoy it.

- **Seed sowing** is a good way of raising many annuals, biennials, vegetables and some perennials. It can also be used for trees and shrubs, but this is very slow. Seeds you buy should be what they say they are, but if you collect your own seeds the results may be less predictable because not all plants come true from seed. For example, if you plant four pips from a single apple you will end up with four completely different trees, each bearing totally different fruit.
- **Division** is mainly used to increase the health and quantity of perennials. Basically, the plant is dug up and divided into smaller parts, which are then replanted to form new plants.

- **Cuttings** can be taken from trees, shrubs and perennials and are particularly useful if you want to reproduce a plant exactly. Depending on the plants, you can take cuttings from roots, hardwood stems, softwood stems or leaf shoots but the principle is always the same: part of the plant is cut off, takes root and forms a new plant exactly the same as the parent.
- **Layering** is a good technique for shrubs with branches that grow close to the ground. It involves burying part of a branch attached to the main plant under the soil to encourage it to grow roots. Some plants, such as ivy, will layer themselves. Once the new roots have established themselves, the branch can be cut off from the main stem and thus a new plant is formed.
- **Grafting** is a method whereby two plants are joined together. It is often used for fruit trees, which do not come true from seed. Depending on the rootstock you use, it enables you to influence the final size of the tree.

The first two methods are the best to start with and are described in more detail below.

Seed sowing

It is remarkably easy to grow many plants from seed. To germinate and grow seeds only need soil, water, warmth and light. It is very satisfying to collect and grow your own seeds but to begin with it is worth buying packets of seeds, as they come with valuable advice for growing that particular plant. The information that follows is applicable to most seeds but planting depths and light requirements can vary considerably. The seed packet should also give you advice on sowing and planting times.

Depending on the plants you are growing and the space you have, you can plant seeds exactly where you want them to grow – in an area of the garden specially set aside for seeds or in containers. Some seedlings (baby plants) do not like being moved so you need to sow them in situ and others need to start in a warm place so they need to be sown in pots or trays. If you have room you can create a nursery bed but you need to ensure the soil is very fine and be aware that slugs and snails will gobble up your young plants given half a chance. Trays, pots, plugs or root trainers are usually the best options. Any container needs good drainage and should hold at least 4 cm/1½ in of soil.

- Trays are fine for starting off seeds but you will need to transplant the seedlings into pots as they get bigger.

- You can buy trays that are divided into individual square compartments, which are useful for small plants.
- Small pots are good but they can take up a lot of space.
- Plugs are small self-contained units of compost that fit into specially-made trays; they are good as the outer covering will naturally disintegrate when you plant them out but you need to watch that they do not dry out.
- Root trainers are trays with long narrow compartments in which you grow the seeds. They are good for plants, such as sweet peas, which have long roots because the roots are trained downwards by the container. When it comes to planting out, the containers split apart so you can get the root ball out without disturbing it too much.

If you are planting your seeds directly into the garden, make sure the soil is broken up to the consistency of fine crumbs and drains well. If you are using a container, you will need to mix soil and compost or buy ready-mixed compost – you cannot use plain garden soil in containers because it is not suitable for such a confined space. You can use specialized seed compost to begin with but you will need to replant the seedlings as they get bigger because it does not contain enough nutrients to support a growing plant. Never re-use compost, even if it looks fine; many of the nutrients will have been used up and it may contain diseases from the previous plant. Vermiculite or perlite is a light volcanic mineral that can be put on top of the compost to stop it drying out or mixed in to make it easier for the new roots to grow.

- Always make sure the compost is damp but drained before planting any seeds and be sure to plant them at the correct depth as specified on the packet.
- Follow any instructions regarding light and temperature; some seeds need a period in darkness to germinate and others need a certain degree of warmth. Many need a relatively humid atmosphere to start with. You can buy trays with lids or you can put a clear plastic bag over the pot and fix it in place with an elastic band. The damp compost will then create the required humidity. The cover should be removed as soon as the seeds start to grow.
- Do not plant too many seeds. Unless you have a very large garden a whole tray of anything will probably be too much.
- Above all do not overwater your seedlings. More than two-thirds of seedlings die from an excess of water. Use a fine rose on a watering can or a mist sprayer.

- Always label everything clearly; most seedlings and many small plants look remarkably similar.
- Once the seedlings grow two or more sets of true leaves (the first pair of leaves to appear as the plant grows are called 'false leaves'), they can be re-potted into larger containers if necessary. Be gentle when doing this as the seedlings will be delicate. You can buy a widger (a small wooden spoon-like tool) to ease the roots up or use a lolly stick or old household spoon.
- If you have grown your seeds indoors, gently adapt the plants to outdoor life by putting them out by day and bringing them in at night. You can increase the amount of time they spend outside gradually over a couple of weeks – start them off in a sheltered spot and bring them in if cold weather is forecast.
- Once the plants are large enough to survive in the open, you can plant them in their permanent positions.

If you are enthusiastic about propagation, you may want to buy a propagator which will allow you to control the heat and humidity. However, do not rush out and buy masses of equipment until you decide whether you really like seed growing.

The following seeds are some of the best to start with: *Alcea* (Hollyhock), *Anchusa*, *Aquilegia*, *Antirrhinum* (Snapdragon), *Campanula pyramidalis* (Chimney bellflower), *Centaurea cyanus* (Cornflower), *Cerinthe*, *Cosmos*, *Dianthus barbatus* (Sweet William), *Digitalis* (Foxglove), *Erisimum cheiri* (Wallflower), *Eschscholzia californica* (Californian poppy), *Helianthus annus* (Sunflower), *Ipomoea* (Morning glory), *Lathyrus odoratus* (Sweet pea), *Lunaria annua* (Honesty), *Myosotis* (Forget-me-not), *Nicotiana* (Tobacco plant), *Nigella* (Love-in-a-mist), *Papaver nudicaule* (Iceland poppy), *Papaver somniferum* (Opium poppy), *Scabious* and *Tropaeolum* (Nasturtium).

Possible problems

If your seeds fail to germinate, the chances are that you have provided the wrong sort of conditions. Seeds you collect yourself are always unpredictable but most packets of seeds from reputable companies should germinate if you follow the instructions. Check you planted them at the correct depth and gave them the correct levels of light and heat and amounts of water.

Once seedlings have grown, their greatest danger is from a disease called 'damping off'. This causes the seedlings to wilt, collapse and eventually die. To prevent this, ensure all containers are thoroughly washed with detergent and well rinsed before using them. Clean your tools, use a fresh compost and use water from the tap rather than that collected in a barrel, which may contain germs that the young plant is not strong enough to fight. Finally, ensure there is enough space between each plant for air to circulate.

Self-seeding

Many garden plants will self-seed naturally as they would in the wild. To encourage this, simply leave the seed heads on the plants and allow nature to do the rest. Obviously, the position and growth of the seedlings will be haphazard, but you can usually successfully move the young plants if they are trying to grow where you do not want them. Seeds from neighbouring gardens may also appear in your garden as a result of wind, birds or animals. Always be careful when you are weeding that you do not pull up future plants you might want.

Division

This is another method of propagation worth considering as it is easy, cost-free and will improve the condition of the plants you already have in your garden. Many perennials that do not have tap roots can be propagated in this way. After three or four years, the plant should have grown considerably and established a large root ball, possibly with an area in the middle that no longer produces many leaves or flowers.

1 The best time to divide perennials is after flowering, when the roots and shoots are just starting to grow. Spring is best for late-flowering plants.
2 Dig the entire plant up gently – use a fork so you do not break too many roots.
3 If necessary wash the earth off the roots using a hose so you can see what you are doing.
4 Some plants, such as geraniums, may develop an unproductive centre as the plant grows outwards. Gently pull the plant apart, remove the middle and divide the rest up to form new plants. Within reason you can divide it as much as you like but you must ensure that each new part has a good 'eye' or growing point. As a general guideline, three or four new plants can usually be made from an established perennial.

5 If the root clump is very congested, you can divide it by using two garden forks. Push both forks into the middle of the root ball, facing away from each other and push apart. Many of the smaller roots will break but this will not matter as long as each part has a reasonable number of roots left.
6 Fleshy roots, such as those of agapanthus, can be divided using a spade or knife. As always, ensure each new plant has a good root to grow from.
7 Replant each section immediately so that the roots do not dry out, and water well.
8 Each section will grow into a new plant, and after a few years you can repeat the process again.

containers

In this chapter you will learn:

- **why every garden should have some containers**
- **the different materials available and their pros and cons**
- **the best plants to choose for containers**
- **how to keep your pots looking good all year round.**

Introduction

Regardless of the size or aspect of your garden, it is worth having some containers. You can grow a great variety of plants in them and the only thing you need to remember is that they will need a little more attention than those plants growing directly in the soil. The advantages are as follows.

- You can grow plants even if you do not have room for a flowerbed.
- You can grow plants that need particular soil such as camellias, which need acid conditions.
- Tender plants can be taken inside during winter or moved to a more protected spot in the garden.
- Containers can provide interest while you are waiting for something to grow up – you can place them either at the edge of the flowerbed or among existing plants within the bed.
- You can move containers around the garden to give seasonal interest.

Almost any plant can be grown in a container as long as the roots have enough room to grow and you provide adequate food and water. Many trees and shrubs will not reach their full size however large the pot is, but this does not necessarily do the plant any harm.

Large containers can be ornaments in their own right and some do not even need to be planted up. As a general rule ornate pots look better with a simple planting scheme of one or two types of plant, whereas plain containers benefit from more varied planting that will draw the eye up and away from the simplicity of the base. When setting up a display of pots it is important to ensure that there is some unifying theme, otherwise the whole area can end up looking a bit of a hotchpotch. Similar-shaped pots of different sizes displayed together look good and a variety of pots made of the same material – like terracotta – can be effective. If you are not satisfied with your display the first time, remember pots can be moved and often easily replanted.

Any object can be used to grow plants in provided it can hold soil and will allow water to drain through it. An enormous variety of purpose-made containers are available. Decide whether you want the pot or the plants within it to be the focal point. If the container is to be the main attraction, you will need to choose it carefully. A pot covered by a mass of ivy and trailing plants need only be a cheap, plain one. Always use the largest container you can; your plants will grow better and the pot will retain water better and be more stable.

Materials

Terracotta

Large terracotta pots are heavy, but this makes them stable and therefore less likely to blow over. Even if it has been fired to a high temperature, unglazed terracotta is nearly always slightly porous. This means water seeps through the container and can cause problems for two reasons. Firstly, the soil may tend to dry out. This can be overcome by lining the pot with plastic or placing a smaller plastic pot inside the terracotta one. When lining the pots, always remember to make plenty of drainage holes at the bottom. Secondly, water seeping into the terracotta in cold weather can cause frost damage. When the water held within the pot freezes, it expands and can cause the pot to crack or even shatter. Containers labelled frost-proof are less likely to suffer from this problem, but no terracotta pot can be 100 per cent frost-proof. In severe winters it is best to protect your pots with lagging (see the 'Winter care' section on page 151). Glazed pots do not suffer from moisture loss but are not always frost-proof.

Stone and fake stone

Genuine antique stone containers can look amazing, but they also tend to be extremely expensive and heavy to move. Fake stone is made of a variety of concrete mixtures, most of which are frost-proof and can be made to age in a similar way to real stone by painting the surface with a coating of sour milk, yogurt or diluted manure.

Timber

All timber needs to be treated otherwise it will eventually rot and fall apart. Every three to five years the container should be emptied, dried and treated with preservative or paint. For this reason it is often easier to plant up a plastic container and put it inside the wooden one so that the plants can be removed easily when necessary. Alternatively, you can line the timber container with polythene to protect it. Barrels used for beer, etc. are sealed, but others may not be. Half barrels make extremely stable planters and are useful for windy sites where other containers might blow over.

Plastic

This is the cheapest form of container, and some can be very attractive and others can be disguised by trailing plants. An important factor to remember is that a bright terracotta pot will fade and mellow whereas a bright plastic pot never will. Plastic containers are also light and may need to be weighted down if in an exposed site. Although it is frost-proof, plastic becomes brittle if exposed to bright sunlight and will eventually crack.

Lead and fibreglass

Lead containers can look beautiful, but tend to be very heavy and expensive. Fibreglass copies are frequently more practical and many are so good that you cannot tell they are fakes until you touch them.

Other materials

You need not restrict yourself to purpose-made containers. Anything that will hold soil and allow water to drain through it can be used. A wicker basket, for example, may only last as a container for a season or two, but could be very attractive. Before you throw away a leaking bucket or old watering can, check first whether it might look good planted up in the garden. If you are using a great variety of containers make sure they go together and do not look like a jumbled mess.

Planting and care

Good drainage is one of the most important factors in successful container gardening, and to facilitate this pots must *always* have drainage holes and should be raised off the ground to allow excess water to drain out of them. You can use bricks for larger pots or terracotta 'feet' for smaller ones. Very large containers that you wish to move around the garden can be put on a slatted wooden base with wheels. This allows drainage and enables the pot to be moved without difficulty.

When you buy a container, always check it has enough drainage holes. They are marked on many plastic troughs, but not pushed out. This can easily be done with any sharp instrument. Holes of 0.5–1 cm/¼–½ in every 10–12 cm/4–5 in are probably adequate for most containers. If you are using a recycled object, like a tin bucket, remember you must make drainage holes in it before planting it up.

You must also ensure that the chosen site is strong enough to support the container. Remember that it will be much heavier when it is full of moist soil and may be unstable if it is in an exposed area. Also be careful when positioning and ensure that the container is not dripped on by gutters or under overhanging trees or other plants.

Large containers are best planted in situ, whereas smaller ones can be filled on a table or workbench. If you are planting up a plastic container that will sit inside something else, always plant it up inside the other pot as the sides of the plastic pot will sag outwards when it is full of soil. This is particularly important for window boxes and long troughs. If you wish to insulate terracotta pots, you need to line them with polythene at this stage, making sufficient drainage holes in the bottom. Otherwise you can use strips of polystyrene or spray-on insulating foam, which will do the same job.

Planting

First, put a layer of stones or broken crocks into the container. This layer must be deep enough to allow the water to soak through without allowing the soil to clog up the drainage holes. The depth will vary according to the size of the container, but 2.5–5 cm/1–2 in is usually sufficient.

Next fill the container with soil. Always use fresh specialist or multi-purpose compost rather than garden soil. If you are only growing annuals and bulbs you may be able to reuse some of the compost but remove all the old roots and add at least half fresh. If you wish to improve the drainage, you can mix in up to a quarter perlite or vermiculite. This will also allow the roots to move with ease through the soil and will lessen the overall weight of the container.

Before you start putting in plants and bulbs, make sure that the soil in the container and around the plants is moist. It is very important that it is not bone dry, but equally it should not be waterlogged. When planting you can also mix in moisture-retaining granules, bone meal and slow-release fertilizer if you wish. The goodness in the compost will only last five to six weeks and after that you will have to provide food for the plants on a regular basis. Plant up to within 1 cm/½ in of the rim of the container. The soil will sink down leaving about 2.5 cm/ 1 in at the top, which allows for a layer of mulch or grit. This looks attractive, prevents evaporation, stops weeds growing and deters slugs and snails. Even if you are not going to use a surface layer, always make sure there is a gap between the surface of the soil and the rim of the container as otherwise any water will simply run off, probably taking the soil with it.

Watering

Plants in containers need more water than those planted directly in the ground as their roots cannot spread out so far and water may be lost via the pot itself. It is possible to install an irrigation system but this is only really useful if you have many pots or if they are situated on exposed balconies or roof gardens and dry out quickly. Irrigation systems are also useful if you go away for long periods in the summer. Otherwise, if this is the case you might be better to plant your garden with fewer containers, and with more drought-tolerant, soil-planted specimens. Watering your containers by hand allows you to judge exactly how much each one needs and to check on the plants as you go around. As a rough guideline, feel the soil 2.5 cm/1 in below the surface – if it is dry you need to water. Moisture meters are available but it is perfectly simple to test by hand.

Moisture-retaining granules can be added at the time of planting. The idea is that they swell up and retain water, which they then release as the soil dries out. It is important to remember that you still need to water – just not as often. Water slowly and gently using a hose or watering can and allow the water time to penetrate the soil properly. Once the soil is saturated, water will start to drain out of the bottom of the pot. If the water falls straight out through the drainage holes the minute you add it, this means the plant has dried out or become pot bound, i.e. the roots have grown too large for the pot. In this case, soak the pot in a bucket with water halfway up the pot's sides and leave it until all the bubbles have stopped rising to the surface. Then re-pot the plant in a larger container with plenty of soil to accommodate the roots.

It is also possible to water plants from the base by sitting them in a dish of water. This is a good method as it allows the plant to take up exactly the amount of water it needs, but you have to be careful as the dish will collect rainwater and the pot may become waterlogged. Dishes are particularly useful if you are going away for the summer. Put the containers close together in a shady, sheltered spot to minimize evaporation and stand the containers in dishes of water.

In winter take care not to overwater containers. Many plants are better able to withstand cold than damp.

Feeding

After about the first six weeks it will be necessary to provide food as well as water for your container plants. A fortnightly feed of liquid seaweed during the growing time will often be sufficient. Tomato food encourages the growth of flowers and is effective when given to annuals. Always follow the instructions as too much food can do as much harm as too little. When feeding, it is important to check that the soil is moist throughout. If in any doubt, water well and feed the next day.

Winter care

Either the container or plant may be unable to withstand cold weather. Bear in mind that some plants, like olive trees, can put up with low temperatures but not a combination of cold and damp. Plants can be protected with sacking or straw wrapped around them or, if necessary, they can be moved indoors. Often moving a container to a more sheltered spot may be sufficient. If you cannot do this and are worried about the container's frost hardiness, wrap it in bubble wrap, sacking or newspaper when temperatures below freezing are forecast.

Hanging baskets

Hanging baskets need slightly different treatment to other containers. They are usually made of wire mesh or plastic and are either free-hanging and circular or wall-mounted and semi-circular. It is worth buying the largest you can as the larger ones hold much more soil and do not dry out so quickly. Depending on the size and situation of your basket, you will need to water it anything from twice a week to twice a day. If you are going away for any length of time, it is worth moving hanging baskets to a shady position. To plant up, see below and Figure 8.1:

1 Balance the basket in a bucket or against the back of a garden chair.
2 Line the basket so the soil will be kept in place. Sphagnum moss looks attractive and allows you to push plants through the base; coconut fibre mats can be cut to fit any basket; or rigid liners made from recycled paper can be bought in most sizes. Rigid liners are the easiest to plant up but you will not be able to grow plants through the mesh of the basket. If using coconut fibre matting, cut and fold it to fit the basket and then cut holes where you wish to put trailing plants. Only make small holes (just large enough to push the plant through) otherwise the earth will fall out. For sphagnum moss, line the basket with moss to a depth of 4 cm/1½ in.
3 Insert the trailing plants through the gaps in the basket and then add a layer of compost.
4 Add fertilizer and perlite or vermiculite to the mixture to provide nutrients and lessen the weight. A handful of each will probably be sufficient for most hanging baskets.
5 Add more trailing plants if you wish around the sides of the basket and then plant up the top.
6 Push the soil down firmly and make sure there is at least 2.5 cm/1 in between the level of the soil and the rim of the basket to allow for watering.

Once it is planted, the basket will be quite heavy so ensure its supports are strong enough. Try to avoid placing the hanging basket in a windy spot as wind dries out the soil even faster than sun.

Window boxes

Window boxes need to be planted up in the same way as any other container, but remember that they need to look good from both inside and outside the house. If you have plastic linings you can remove one lining, as soon as the plants start to fade and replace it with a new set of planting in a second lining. This method allows bulbs to die back naturally and also enables you to grow plants from seed in the containers before putting them on display. While they are out of use, the plastic liners can be kept in a less noticeable part of the garden. Make sure all of your window boxes have adequate drainage and are firmly secured in place.

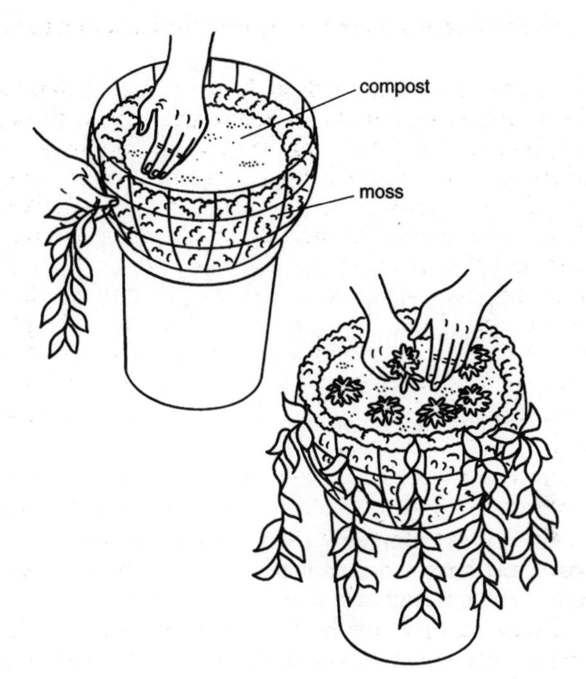

figure 8.1 it is easiest to plant up a hanging basket if you wedge it in the top of a bucket. Push plants through the side of the basket as you work your way up, planting the top last. Allow a gap of at least 3 cm/1½ in between the surface of the compost and the rim of the basket

Plants

Most containers are planted with a mixture of plant types such as perennials, bulbs, annuals and maybe even a shrub or tree.

Annuals

Annuals are brilliant in containers, either on their own or combined with permanent plantings. They are an easy way to maintain seasonal interest and can be used to fill any gaps. As they are only short lived, it does not matter that their roots are restricted, and many will grow in tiny pots.

Alpines

Alpines do particularly well in containers because it is possible to mimic the thin well-drained soil they are used to in their natural habitats. Any container with good drainage works well, but large sinks and stone troughs are particularly effective because they show off the little plants to great advantage. Rocks can be added to make the result look more natural. Put about one-third of pebbles or broken crocks in the bottom of the container to ensure really good drainage. The planting mixture should be half grit and half potting compost. Once you have planted up the container, add another layer of grit on the surface to deter slugs and snails. Try to give the container a really good soaking when it is dry, rather than watering little and often, as this will mimic the mountain storms that the plants thrive in.

Perennials

Perennials are not as commonly used in containers as annuals and shrubs. Most have a dormant period when they die down or need to be cut back, and they do not look so attractive during this time. However, they can be useful in large containers to form part of a year-round planting scheme where other plants, such as shrubs or bulbs, will provide interest while the perennials are dormant.

Bulbs

These all do well in containers and can be densely planted. Bulbs are useful because they can provide flowers from late winter to late autumn and do not take up much room.

Grasses

Grasses are very good specimen plants and a single grass may be all you need in a particularly ornate container. Many look good throughout winter.

Shrubs

Shrubs will often grow perfectly happily in containers although not all will reach their full size. Ideally the container should be a quarter to a third as tall as the final height of the plant and roughly the same diameter. You should use specialist tree and shrub compost as this will provide the necessary nutrients to get the plant started. You need to feed during the growing season and water as necessary throughout the year. Climbers can also be grown successfully in containers, but the container should be as large as possible.

Trees

Trees can be successfully grown in containers but most will not reach their full size and will not live as long as they would if planted in the ground. The container should be a minimum of 50 cm/20 in deep and wide. When planting, use specialist tree and shrub compost and allow 8 cm/3 in between the surface of the soil and the edge of the pot. This gap will allow you to soak the plant thoroughly when you water it. It is important to water trees in containers regularly and to ensure that the water penetrates right to the bottom of the container. The best way to do this is to water the tree once a week with a generous amount so that the soil is really soaked rather than giving it a little every day. Any of the trees listed in Chapter 05 (page 59) would be suitable.

Herbs

Herbs can easily be grown in containers and in fact many grow better this way as it is easier to provide the well-drained soil they like. Mint is best grown in a container because it is highly invasive. See the 'Herbs' section in Chapter 09 for cultivation.

Fruit

Fruit trees are now frequently available on dwarf rootstock and these can be successfully grown in containers. Apple, cherry, quince and fig are all possibilities, fig being particularly suitable as it grows best when its roots are constricted. Currant and gooseberry bushes can be grown in containers, but the most successful container fruits of all are strawberries. Strawberry pots gently curve upwards and have openings up the sides. This enables you to grow plants all over the pot and gives the strawberries the maximum chance to reach the sun and ripen.

Vegetables

Vegetables can be grown in containers and, as they warm up sooner than the soil, you may get an early crop. Cultivation of vegetables is covered in Chapter 09 (see page 161), but potatoes, beans, ruby chard and tomatoes all do especially well in containers.

the kitchen garden

In this chapter you will learn:

- **how to plan a kitchen garden**
- **how to grow really tasty vegetables**
- **the best ways to get perfect fruit**
- **about growing all the herbs you'll want for your kitchen.**

Introduction

Anyone can grow at least some of their own produce. This has recently become very popular: home-grown produce tastes better and fits in with modern concepts of local food, organic production and sustainability. Good home-grown organic produce is healthier for you than its non-organic equivalent and is far preferable in terms of food kilometres/miles than imported fruit and vegetables. If you take trouble to grow your own fruit and vegetables you won't want to eat them if they have been treated regularly with long-lasting chemicals strong enough to kill off pests and diseases. This chapter tells you how to get started and concentrates on the basic principles of growing vegetables, fruit and herbs, giving advice on what to do and how to do it.

You can grow some fruit, vegetables and herbs in boxes or containers. However, kitchen gardening – though satisfying – is harder work than growing flowers, needing more time and effort with regular care and attention. For good yields you need good initial conditions and a control of pests and diseases. Occasionally, you can lose an entire crop of something to a disease – then you need to be quite philosophical.

When you start out, concentrate on the easier crops. For example, a good crop of courgettes (which really only need freedom from frost, good soil, sun, plenty of water and regular feeding) is much easier to produce than prize cauliflowers (which seem to need 24-hour intensive care from a team of experts). To begin with, concentrate on food that:

- is not too difficult
- you really like eating
- would be expensive to buy or difficult to find in the shops
- fits in with the rest of your garden.

Planning your site

Any area of your garden that is set aside just for growing food needs to be carefully chosen. It should be sunny, have fairly good well-drained soil, be sheltered from the wind and easy to water. The old walled kitchen gardens were designed on these principles and also kept out rabbits and other animals who would have liked their share of the food! Herbs are best grown somewhere sunny (pots and containers are practical and look good) near the kitchen so they are accessible for cooking.

The same goes for salad crops, which you can also grow in raised beds to reduce the slug problem.

Crop rotation

Vegetables do better when grown in different places each year – this reduces concentrations of pests and diseases and improves the balance of soil nutrients. This is called 'crop rotation' – groups of plants are moved between different areas over a three-year period (see Figure 9.1). Woody-stemmed plants, such as trees and fruit bushes, cannot be moved around in this way and one or two vegetables, such as asparagus and Jerusalem artichokes, need to stay in the same place over their entire life cycle. Moveable crops fall into three groups (see Figure 9.1):

1 Legumes (peas and beans).
2 'Cabbagey' crops called 'brassicas'.
3 Root vegetables.

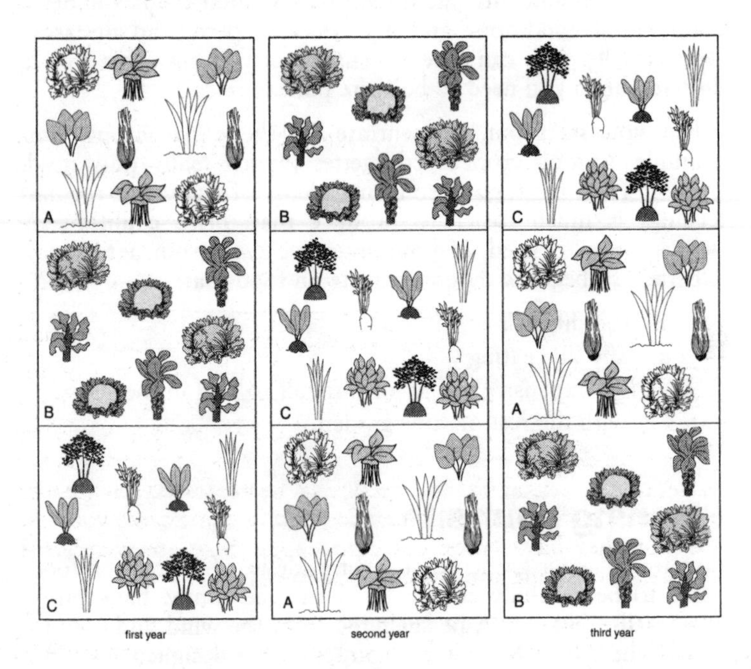

figure 9.1 simple three-bed rotation. A: peas and beans (called 'legumes') can be planted with celery, courgettes, leeks, lettuce, marrows, onions, spinach and tomatoes. B: Brassicas such as broccoli, Brussels sprouts, cabbage, calabrese, cauliflower and kale. C: Root vegetables, such as beetroot, carrots, parsnips and potatoes

In theory, you divide the ground into equal portions and move the different types of crops so they occupy a different space in each of the three years. In practice you won't grow equal amounts of each, so do what you can.

Keep records of what you did when (a handwritten diary, computerized notes or dated digital photographs) to remind you what was planted where, when and how well it worked. Dated photographs of frost-struck courgettes planted too early, or dried-up and unwatered peas in a drought suggest what to avoid next year. Look at wind and rain patterns, where shadows fall during the day, and areas rain doesn't reach (because of something like a wall or big tree). For best access in all sorts of weather, try using narrow, possibly raised, beds reached from paths. Weeding and picking, etc. become easier but the building takes time and costs money. Otherwise, grow fruit and vegetables among your flowers. Carefully arranged, this can look decorative – most of the formal planting at the Chateau de Villandry in France is composed of vegetables and fruit trees set within borders of box. This method avoids large tempting concentrations of tasty food (monocultures) that are more vulnerable to pests and diseases.

Vegetables can give huge visual pleasure, even if separated from the rest of the garden. If you want to do more than grow food there is plenty of potential to use an artistic temperament and talent. Squashes, small pumpkins, beans and peas grown up arrangements of canes (like the traditional rows of runner beans) introduce height and verticality. Use tepees in the same way and to support flowers like nasturtiums or sweet peas. Many vegetables' flowers are coloured (yellow in courgettes and squashes; reds, oranges, pinks and even blues in beans) as are some of the produce (different beans come in reds, blues and yellows as well as green). Make use of interesting outlines (lovage and sweetcorn, for example). Old and traditional varieties of vegetables are becoming more widely available. Some are delicious, some interesting and in some cases you can see why they have fallen out of use, but there are wonderful variations of shape and colour to be found.

Fruit trees have four seasons of interest: outline in winter (especially if trained into clever shapes), blossom in spring (with fragrance), leaf and shape in summer, and the ripening fruit in autumn.

Containers

Many fruits and vegetables (and especially herbs) can be grown successfully in containers. Specialist growing bags are available for many vegetables: although ugly they are easily disguised – courgette foliage or other crops' leaves will hide them, or put a row of low containers of herbs or annuals in front of the bags. Provided the containers are deep enough for the roots then beans, carrots, courgettes, lettuce, potatoes and tomatoes do well in them but they will still need regular feeding and watering, like anything else grown in this way. Most fruits need large containers in order to flourish (see the 'Shrubs' and 'Trees' sections in Chapter 08) and a lot of care and attention. However, strawberries thrive so well in compact containers that special ones have been designed just for them.

Problems

Kitchen garden pests and diseases are usually more serious than those affecting flowers. Roses will probably survive and bloom even with greenfly, but if slugs eat your lettuce there will be nothing left for you! Since spraying your crops with powerful chemicals is not a good idea, you need to use care and ingenuity instead. For example:

- Put each crop where it will grow best.
- Do not plant too close together (fungal diseases specially spread faster in these conditions).
- Watch your plants carefully to spot problems early on.
- Planting crops in conjunction with 'companion' plants that reduce their vulnerability to pests (see page 162).
- Net fruit to prevent birds eating it.
- Remove dead, diseased and damaged branches from fruit trees during pruning and keep the centre of the tree open.
- Cover plants with horticultural fleece to thwart insect pests – this looks ugly but usually works for brassicas, like cabbages, salads, like rocket, and carrots and parsnips.
- Remove diseased parts of plants immediately so the disease doesn't spread.
- Remedy nutritional deficiencies immediately.
- Control slugs (see 'Pests, disease and weeds' in Chapter 07). Biological controls can be effective against pests.

Vegetables

In the right place, vegetables will more than repay necessary care and attention, and a packet of seeds can be transformed into a series of delicious meals. When planning what to plant, it helps to classify vegetables according to the part you actually eat.

- **Leaves and salad** – this includes cabbages, lettuce and rocket, as well as numerous crops such as kale and ruby chard, which combine decorative potential with good eating characteristics.
- **Fruits and flowers** – this includes some brassicas, like broccoli and cauliflowers, and the entire cucurbit family, from Central and South America, of tomatoes, cucumber, squashes, pumpkins and courgettes. These vegetables don't like frost and should not be planted out until the danger has passed, and this is the same for many other interesting and attractive plants including cardoons, aubergines, peppers and sweetcorn. Some perennials, like asparagus and artichokes, need permanent beds.
- **Pods** – this includes peas and beans, which can often be grown vertically, needing little ground and frequently having interestingly coloured flowers and pods.
- **Bulbs, stems and roots** – these form much of the basic stock of the vegetable garden and include onions, garlic, potatoes, carrots and parsnips.

Sowing and planting

As most vegetables are annuals, you can choose new varieties to grow every year. New strains are being developed all the time and often include improved disease resistance among their properties.

Split crops into hardy ones that can be planted out while there is still a danger of frost (although everything does better when the ground is warmer) and those that are frost-tender. A good way to get started with frost-tender plants is to buy individual plants in pots at a garden centre and then plant them out: tomatoes, courgettes and sweetcorn will give you a satisfying yield from a few plants. As you become more experienced, you may find a suitable location (like a greenhouse) to bring the plants on from seeds.

Peas and broad beans are best started from seed planted into the ground, although with runner beans and French beans you may grow them on from seed in pots until the ground has warmed up. Carrots and parsnips, with their long roots, have to be started from seed planted where they will grow to maturity.

With a little careful planning, you can enjoy fresh vegetables throughout the year, extending the growing season by providing protection to seedlings from cold and wind using traditional cloches, horticultural fleece or polytunnels. Fleece or perforated plastic needs to be weighted down at the edges after being gently draped over the plants. Polytunnels need circular hoops every 30 cm/12 in and need to be fixed to a stake at either end. They can suffer from build-ups of condensation and don't look very pretty, but they are cheap and a cost-effective way of providing protection to plants that need it. Cloches can be improvised using the cut-off ends of plastic bottles for individual plants or fixing discarded windows on simple block work frames for larger areas. Remember the safety aspects before you start on this, and to supply adequate ventilation.

Companion planting

This provides an effective method to improve your produce since some plant combinations deter pests, combat diseases or improve soil; others work badly and Table 9.1 gives examples of both.

table 9.1 companion planting

Crop	Good combination	Bad combination
Beans	Spinach, brassicas	Onions, garlic and sunflowers
Brassicas	Parsley, chrysanthemums	Onions, garlic, rue, strawberries
Carrots	Onions, garlic, rosemary, sage, chives, lettuce, tomatoes, radishes, marigolds	
Courgettes	Sweetcorn, peas, beans	Potatoes, brassicas
Lettuce	Carrots, strawberries	
Onions	Carrots, brassicas, tomatoes, leeks, lettuce, chamomile	Beans
Peas	Beans, carrots, leeks, turnips, parsley and herbs generally	Onions and garlic
Potatoes	Beans, marigolds, strawberries	Tomatoes, apples, sunflowers

Radishes	Chervil, nasturtiums, lettuce, peas	Brassicas, spinach
Tomatoes	French marigolds, basil, carrots, onions, garlic, nasturtiums, parsley, nettles	Brassicas, potatoes, fennel

Planting distances

Planting distances should be given on the seed packet or pot at the time you buy them, but can be adapted to fit your available ground. If you shorten planting distances be careful with watering and feeding and look out for diseases.

Intercropping

This is a method of planting that allows you to grow two crops in one space, for example, a fast- and a slow-growing one (lettuce and radishes between carrots and parsnips, or broad beans with potatoes). Companion planting and intercropping can work together – red onions planted at intervals in rows of carrots will help deter carrot fly, look decorative and taste good.

For vegetables that will sprout again, such as spinach and some lettuce, you can remove some of the leaves and let the rest grow on, increasing the yield. It works well for salad crops in raised beds.

Watering

Watering is essential for successful vegetable growing, and not only at times of planting and sowing. Without adequate water, plants have a tendency to bolt – that is, in anticipation of a drought, they speed up their growth to produce flowers and seeds and complete their life cycle as fast as possible, whereas you want to prolong the growing period as long as possible.

Weeding

Weeding is as important as watering. The delicate new seedlings must be kept clear of weeds to make maximum use of available food and water and to avoid being choked by the competition. At first this has to be done by hand but, later, crops planted in straight lines can be hoed between rows.

Table 9.2 summarizes the best ways to grow individual crops.

table 9.2 vegetables: planting, care and harvesting

Vegetables	Planting	Care	Harvesting	Problems	Notes
Broccoli and calabrese	Sunny site and moist soil. Start with seeds planted in trays in mid-spring and transplant in early/midsummer 60 cm/24 in apart. Stagger planting to provide autumn and winter crops.	Water well, weed and feed after the first head has been harvested. Sprouting broccoli may need the stems shored up with earth if the heads become top heavy.	Cut central head first and then smaller side heads as they grow – they will reduce in size as the season goes by.	Cabbage root fly, club root, caterpillars and birds.	Calabrese should be planted in situ two or three seeds 15 cm/6 in apart and then thinned. Romanesco is particularly good.
Broad beans	Well-manured, heavy but not waterlogged soil. Sow late autumn ('Aquadulce Claudia') or winter onwards 5 cm/ 2 in deep and 23 cm/9 in apart.	Need to be supported (e.g. by canes and string). Don't allow them to dry out once the flowers have formed.	Summer when the pods are still small and the beans just showing through.	Aphids	'Aquadulce Claudia' is the best single broad bean and can be sown in late autumn for cropping the next year. 'Bunyard's Exhibition' is a good later variety.

Vegetables	Planting	Care	Harvesting	Problems	Notes
Carrots	Sunny and sheltered site. Carrots do best in light sandy soil and need to be sowed once the ground has warmed up (> 7 °C) in mid-spring. Mix the seed with sand and try to sow 7.5 cm/3 in apart.	Weed and water gently, feeding once the seedlings appear.	Summer to mid-winter. Lift by hand or with a fork and keep soil mulched in winter so it remains malleable.	Carrot fly.	Avoid thinning and interplant with onions to deter carrot fly. Use fleece.
Courgettes (Zucchini)	Sunny sheltered site. Either sow in spring in pots for later transplanting or transplant bought plants in early summer once the danger of frost has passed.	Feed every two weeks and water well once flowers appear. Too much water before will only encourage leaves.	Midsummer to late autumn. Taste best about 10cm/4 in long.	Aphids and slugs.	Fruits will wither without enough food and water.

Vegetables	Planting	Care	Harvesting	Problems	Notes
French beans	Rich soil and a sheltered but sunny site. Sow seeds either in pots for later transplanting or in situ 22 cm/9 in apart in late spring to midsummer. The soil needs to have reached 12 °C before seeds or plants go in.	Provide support to taller types, mulch to avoid weeds, and water well especially when flowering.	Midsummer to mid-autumn, picking when 10 cm/4 in long. Haricot beans should be left on the pod and the whole plant cut and brought indoors to dry once the pods are grown.	Slugs, black bean aphids and red spider mites together with grey mould in damp conditions.	Dwarf varieties can be fiddly to pick. The wide range of colours in both flower and pods (green, yellow and purple) add to the pleasure in using these plants.
Lettuce	Good drainage and sun or partial shade. Sow 1 cm/ $^1/_2$ in deep and thin when seedlings appear and again at four weeks. Sow in succession at ten-day intervals.	Feed every three to four weeks and water in the mornings to let the leaves dry off and avoid mildew.	Can eat second thinning. Harvest regularly – they don't keep once ripe. Earliest crop within four weeks of sowing.	Aphids, slugs and birds. Bolting or tip burn due to lack of water and mildew from too much.	Types are available for most seasons with a wide range of colour and leaf, so interesting possibilities throughout the year. Choose strains resistant to grey mould.

Vegetables	Planting	Care	Harvesting	Problems	Notes
Onions	Fertile soil, good drainage and sun. Plant sets (specially treated small onions) so tops are just visible and 10 cm/4 in apart. You can also grow from seed in trays and transplant, or from seed in situ in early or mid-spring.	Weed and water if dry. Push the sets back into the soil if birds lift them.	Ready when the leaves are dry and bend over, usually early autumn onwards.	Onion fly.	If the soil is poor then sets are better and mature quicker, although the range is limited and they cost rather more.
Peas	Moist soil, sun or partial shade. Sow in succession in early spring to midsummer using appropriate varieties – known as early, second early, and maincrops.	Grow up framework of pea sticks. Mulch. Feed at seedling stage and water well when in flower.	Pick at regular intervals to encourage growth.	Net against birds. Mice. Some strains are resistant to fusarium wilt and mildew.	Smooth-seeded varieties are tougher (grow early and late in season) but the wrinkle-seeded varieties tend to taste sweeter.

Vegetables	Planting	Care	Harvesting	Problems	Notes
Potatoes	Moist, slightly acidic soil is best with manure or compost dug in just before planting. Leave seed potatoes on trays indoors to sprout for a month before planting, which should take place about one month before the likely date of the last frost. 10 cm/4 in deep, 30 cm/2 in apart and 60 cm/24 in between rows.	Water and feed plants when young and pile up earth around base as necessary to prevent the potatoes showing above ground.	Earlies planted early to mid-spring to crop mid summer, followed by second earlies. Maincrops planted in mid- to late spring and crop mid-autumn. Dig up the whole plant gently with a fork.	Scab develops if too little water given and blight (grow resistant varieties) can affect later crops especially in damp weather. Eelworms.	Use only specially developed seed potatoes to reduce risk of disease. Growing times range from 15 weeks for earlies to 19 weeks for maincrops.

Vegetables	Planting	Care	Harvesting	Problems	Notes
Radishes	Best in light soil (like carrots) and partial shade. Sow 1 cm/$^1/_2$ in deep and 15 cm/6 in apart at two-week intervals from early spring to early autumn.	Water regularly.	Late spring onwards with winter varieties being slower to mature (midsummer to mid-winter).	Slugs.	Oval shapes in red, green, black, purple and yellow. Mooli and Daikon are long, white winter varieties.
Rocket, Roquette, Rugola, Arugola	Any soil, partial shade. Sow in succession every two weeks from early spring to late summer (only as much as you will eat), subsequently thinning seedlings to 15 cm/6 in apart.	Water, weed and feed regularly.	Cut leaves 3 cm/ $1^1/_2$ in above soil and new leaves will grow.	Flea beetle (use fleece).	Do not confuse edible rocket (*Eruca vesicaria*) with sweet rocket (*Hesperis matronalis*).

Vegetables	Planting	Care	Harvesting	Problems	Notes
Runner beans	Moist well-composted soil in full or partial shade. Sow seeds in pairs, either in siitu in late spring 10 cm/4 in apart or in pots, for planting out in early summer.	Provide support, and feed at seedling stage. Mulch and water well especially when in flower.	Late summer to mid-autumn, picking when 10–15 cm/4–6 in long.	Slugs, black bean aphids, red spider mites and pollen beetles.	Tall, dwarf and stringless varieties all available.
Tomatoes	Fertile soil and sheltered sunny site – a south facing wall is ideal. Sow seeds indoors early to mid-spring, hardening off and planting out when the soil reaches 10 °C. They can be either cordons (one main stem) planted 38–45 cm/15–18 in apart or bushes, at least 60 cm/24 in apart.	Mulch. Water but not so much as to split the fruit – around 10 litres/2.2 gallons per week once the flowers appear when you can also feed with specialist tomato food following instructions. With cordons stake them firmly and pinch out side and top shoots to maintain the shape and height you want.	Remove ripe fruits gently in late summer and autumn. Bring all fruits in before the first frost to finish ripening indoors.	Slugs, potato blight if grown near potatoes or in very wet weather. Various specific diseases such as blossom end rot.	Cordons are climbing plants needing support, while bushes are free standing but need a mulch of straw to stop the fruit rotting on touching the soil. Some varieties do much better under glass. A good all-round outside plant is 'Gardener's Delight'. Some old varieties are lovely but can be tricky.

Fruit

Fruit is often divided into:

- tree (top) fruit, such as apples, pears, plums and cherries, and other less common varieties, such as quinces, figs, mulberries, and the tender peaches and apricots.
- soft fruit, such as the deciduous strawberries, or woody bushes and canes, such as raspberries, blackcurrants, redcurrants and gooseberries.

People worry fruit will take up space (not necessarily so), needs time to develop (true for trees) and is difficult (sometimes it is, but it is equally rewarding).

Most fruit will be around for a long time and is hard to move once planted so find the right place first time – sunny with good soil, sheltered, clear of weeds and preferably not vulnerable to frost, which can kill early blossom. If you can't find a good site, it isn't worth planting tree fruit although smaller varieties grown on 'dwarfing' root systems work in containers. Soft fruit is less fussy: most performs reasonably in light shade, and strawberries do well in containers.

Many problems can be resolved with common sense and good practice, but fruit can't be rotated yearly like vegetables so unfortunately it is more vulnerable to pests, diseases and soil conditions.

- Good sites prevent many problems.
- Fruit is generally vulnerable to deficiencies of nutrients so soil condition is vital.
- All fruit needs a regular supply of water and will not perform well without it. Mulching is increasingly important to control evaporation as the climate changes.
- Soft fruit blossom can be protected from frost by covering it with horticultural fleece at critical times. Early blossoming fruit trees, like pears, are at considerable risk in frosty regions. Choose a suitable variety or grow something else!
- Tree fruit crops need to be thinned out when the fruits are small, usually in June, to save you having lots of small, not very nice fruit! Most amateur gardeners hate doing it but it really works.
- Some pruning is necessary. It is quite simple and much easier than many 'experts' say.
- Harvest little, often and carefully.

- Fruit is prone to pests and diseases, but you can do quite a lot to avoid and control them. Net soft fruit against birds if you want most of the crop left for you. Strawberries are vulnerable to slugs but mulches are effective. Consider disease-resistant varieties.
- Yields depend on age. Most fruit trees need to have their roots and main branch structure established before they produce much fruit. It can take four or more years to harvest a decent crop, which will eventually decline as the tree ages. Soft fruit usually won't produce much fruit from bushes or canes in the first year, and has an effective life of between seven and ten years at full production. Strawberries start quickly but decline after three years.

Tree fruit

Tree or 'top' fruit grows on a hardwood tree. This section concentrates on apples, pears, plums and cherries with short notes on the other tree fruit. See 'Taking it further' to find out more about these and other fruit trees.

Try to buy trees from a specialist supplier. Explain carefully about their intended purpose and position to avoid spending time and effort on something unsuitable. Fruit trees do not come true from seed or pips. Most fruit trees are 'grafted' or joined on to the root system (rootstock) of another suitable fruit tree just above ground level leaving a bulge called the 'graft' or 'union'. The chosen rootstocks influence the size and growing properties of the resulting tree: when you buy a tree check it is growing on a suitable rootstock for your requirements.

Most fruit is evenly distributed along the side branches on little clusters known as 'spurs' – the fruit buds are called 'spur bearers'. Some trees only form fruit buds at the end of the branches ('tip bearers') – if you prune the ends of all these branches in the winter you won't get any fruit the following year!

Pruning can be surrounded by mystique, but most of it is common sense. Cut off dead, diseased and damaged wood. Keep a good shape to pick the fruit from and a supply of fruiting wood. Basic pruning techniques are covered in Chapter 07 (page 127). Pruning when the tree is young is intended to form a strong framework. Once shaped (four years old and onwards), the aim is to balance old and new growth while keeping the tree healthy. Most pruning of apples and pears is carried out in winter when the tree is dormant, but plums and cherries must be pruned earlier to discourage a disease called 'Silver Leaf'.

Free-standing trees are usually grown as 'bushes' with three to five sideways branches coming off the trunk around knee height and the central stem cut out above this point. You cannot mow or walk under these but the fruit is easy to pick. Taller 'half standards' or 'standards' have longer sections of bare trunk before the branches begin.

Trees can also be grown against a wall or supported on a framework of stretched wires. The most useful shape for beginners is called a 'cordon': growth is concentrated on a single stem at 45° to the ground, taking up very little space – ideal for small gardens. Additional pruning is needed in summer to keep the trees' shape.

General planting of trees is covered in Chapter 07 (page 107). Heed grower's advice on planting distances and avoid positions where other fruit trees previously grew.

Many fruit trees are not self-pollinating and two or more compatible trees are needed for a crop of fruit to form successfully. The grower can advise you about this and whether, for example, you will need another tree to plant alongside yours.

All trees needs need regular watering in the first year, a spring mulch and regular weeding around the base. Check the tie and stake frequently. Remove blossom in the first year to channel the tree's energy into a strong framework. Thin the crop in June so the branches are not over weighted with fruit once it matures. Once fruit begins to fall from the tree, it is generally ready for picking – gently twist it away from the stalk using a cupped hand. If it doesn't come away easily, it isn't ready. Apples can be stored in cool dry conditions, not touching each other.

With only a few trees you can control many problems by looking after them well, keeping them regularly fed and watered, and removing any ailing or damaged growth immediately. The strong chemicals used by commercial growers are not things you would want to have in your garden or your body. Birds can be a problem, occasionally stripping the buds, but unless your trees are very small it is impractical to net them.

For most common tree fruit, methods of cultivation are similar but there are still some significant differences, as detailed below.

- **Apples** often do particularly well close to the area in which they were bred. 'Blenheim Orange', for example, thrives near Oxford, England while some whose taste you may enjoy (e.g. 'Cox's Orange Pippin') are not easy to grow. Take advice from a specialist grower – there are thousands of little-known varieties, many with excellent flavour.
- **Pears** are more vulnerable to frost than apples so many varieties are unsuitable in cold areas, although again there are local exceptions. There are far fewer varieties of pears than of apple. If they settle down, they will live for a very long time, but the fruit doesn't store well.
- **Plums** seem to need more warmth than other fruit so give them the sunniest spot you have – both 'Victoria' and 'Marjorie's Seedling' are good varieties. All plums and cherries should be pruned in spring or late summer, not in winter.
- **Cherries** tend to grow too big for small gardens unless you grow the bitter Morello variety, although recently some smaller types have been developed. Birds are very keen to get the fruit!

You may come across other tree fruit: quinces and medlars have beautiful decorative blossom and are greatly underappreciated although the fruit needs to be cooked before eating. Mulberries take up quite a lot of space and figs need a warm site and a restricted root run. Peaches, apricots and nectarines are generally frost-tender unless greenhouse grown, although you might be lucky on a warm wall. See 'Taking it further' (page 193) for more information on all these.

Soft fruit

Soft fruit is divided into strawberries (which are low growing and die down each winter), and canes and bushes of permanent plants. Strawberries are easy to grow (unless the year is very wet) and offer quick rewards, so they would usually be the first choice for beginners. Other soft fruit needs rather longer to become established and deserves careful pruning to give you the best results. Canes also need support on some sort of trellis.

All soft fruit needs continuous care during the growing season to obtain a good crop. Netting is essential (except for blackberries) unless you want to lose much to the birds (see Figure 9.2). Canes can be netted over their supporting trellis, for other plants you can buy aluminium fruit cages or make your own from wooden posts fixed around the edge of the area and chicken-wire. Remember to leave a flap so that you can get in and out! It is simpler to use tall cane uprights (2 m/6 ft) at the edges of the bed, with a flowerpot on the top of each and the netting draped over them and weighted down with rocks or bricks on the ground.

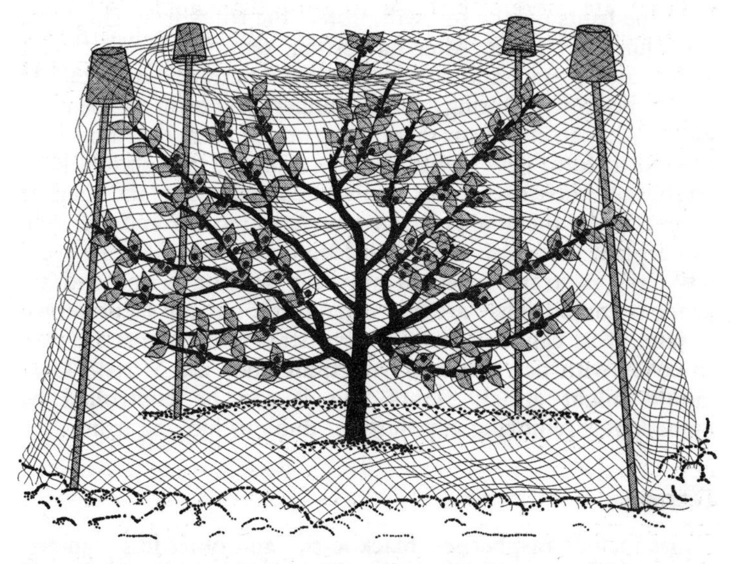

figure 9.2 a net such as this is useful to protect soft fruit

Strawberries

Unlike other soft fruits, strawberries have no woody growth. By planting a mixture of summer and perpetual strawberries you can have fruits from late spring to late autumn. They need some shelter, sun or light shade and like rich, heavy, weed-free soil. Add plenty of compost when preparing the bed. Strawberries do not do well on chalk or soil that has had potatoes, chrysanthemums, tomatoes or other strawberries growing in it during the previous three years. Summer fruiting types should be planted in the late summer or early autumn, and perpetual plants in autumn or spring. Plants grown in containers, such as special strawberry pots, can be planted at any time as long as the weather is mild.

When planting, leave 45 cm/18 in between plants in the ground with the crown of the plant just above ground level.

The plants usually live for three to five years and need to be rotated after this time, which prevents soil exhaustion and the establishment of disease. Feed them with potash, and water well during the growing season – don't get water on the fruits as they ripen since this makes them more likely to rot.

Mulching around the plants with straw or strawberry mats to keep the fruits off the soil will protect the fruits from slugs and rot while they ripen. After harvesting, remove the old foliage and straw or mats and cut the stems down to about 8 cm/3 in above the crown. During growth, runners will form off the main plant. You can either cut them away or peg them down into the ground to form new plants. By late summer, they should have established their own roots and you can cut the plant from its parent. Leave the new plant for a week to recover and then you can replant it for use next year. Ideally, harvest the fruit every few days as strawberries do not keep well once ripe and are prone to mould. They are best eaten fresh, but can be preserved as jam. Frost can be a problem, but strawberry plants are easy to cover with newspaper if you think they are at risk. Grey mould might attack plants, but it can be controlled by immediately removing any fluffy or dubious looking fruit.

Canes

Canes include raspberries, blackberries and other less common fruits such as loganberries and tayberries. They generally do not grow well on chalk or windy sites: they do best on rich, slightly acidic soil in sun or light shade and need watering in summer. After planting, cut the stems back to 23 cm/9 in to encourage new growth. Except for the prolific blackberries, cane fruits need to be netted against birds. Their spiny flexible canes (hence the name) really need to be supported on a single- or double-trellis framework. A system of single or, preferably doubled posts (see Figure 9.3) 3 m/10 ft apart with three strands of strong wire stretched in between them at heights of 75 cm/2½ ft, 1.1 m/3½ ft and 1.5 m/5 ft provides the basis. Extra twine woven between the wires helps train the fruit.

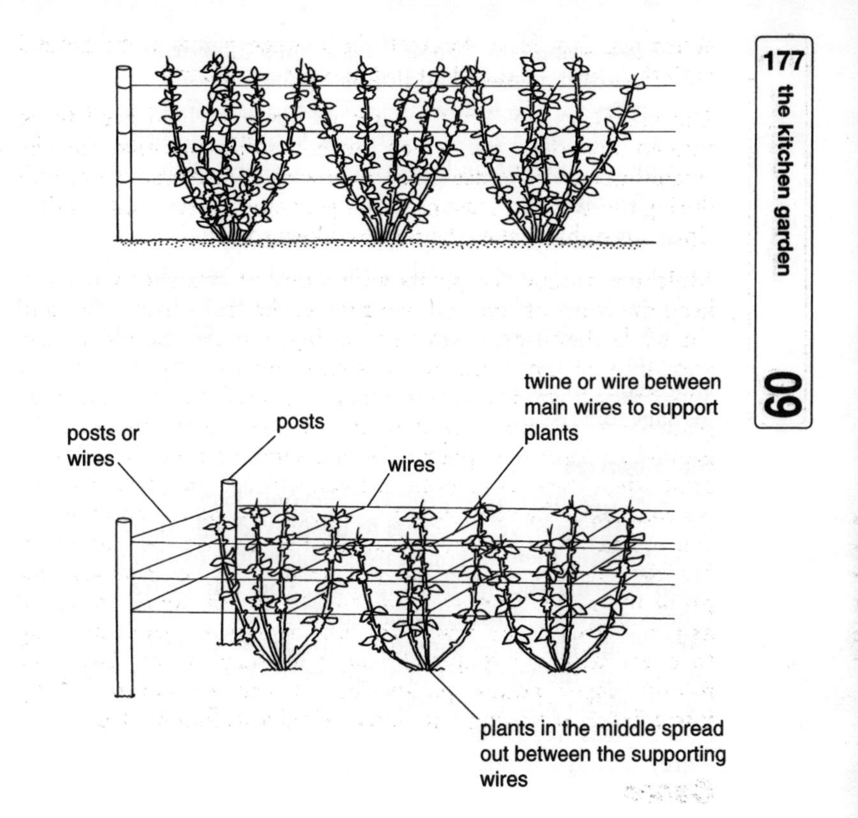

figure 9.3 trellis for cane fruit

Raspberries

Raspberries are so delicious that it is worth taking the trouble to grow them. There are two main types – summer and autumn fruiting. Raspberries should be planted in late autumn 60 cm/ 24 in apart. Mulch in early spring with a non-limey mulch (i.e. not alkaline mushroom compost). Carefully pull up any suckers.

The autumn-fruiting raspberry plant grows densely, takes up more room than the summer-fruiting plant, but provides fruit at an unusual time and is not so attractive to birds. It is also easy to prune – just cut the fruited canes to the ground once the harvest is over and new ones will grow for next year.

Summer-fruiting canes should be pruned after fruiting, cutting old canes to the ground and thinning the new one. Leave six or eight canes for the following year's crop as raspberries fruit on the previous year's growth. After the winter trim the top of each cane by a couple of buds – pruning is easiest if they are grown in a fan shape.

Summer fruits should be ready in mid- to late summer and autumn fruits in early to mid-autumn. They should be dry when picked and should come away easily. They do not keep well and should be eaten or processed within hours of picking. Virus-resistant varieties are now widely available so, if possible, choose one of these. Cane spot and raspberry beetle maggots are manageable risks.

Blackberries

Blackberries have few problems beyond keeping them under control. If you have no access to unsprayed wild ones, you may want to plant them in your garden – any time from late autumn to early spring and 3.5 m/12 ft apart. They can be trained along canes or grown through a hedge. Cut out fruited canes after harvesting. The fruits should be ripe in early autumn, coming away from the stem without difficulty. The earliest fruits are usually better and the fruits no longer taste good after the first frosts. Virus-free plants are available and the only real problem – grey mould – is not that common.

Bushes

Although fruit bushes take a little time to become established and need attention and netting, the taste of home-grown gooseberries, redcurrants and white currants (all of which grow on a single stem) or blackcurrants (growing on a group of stems) is so delicious you may well decide to grow them. Green and red gooseberries, for example, are totally different from the fruits usually available in shops as you can (unlike commercial gooseberries) wait to harvest them when they are perfectly ripe.

All bush fruit does best on well-drained, but not dry, soil in moderate, damp climates with enough sun to ripen the fruit. Avoid frosty and windy sites. Typically, bushes should be set around 1.2–1.5 m/4–5 ft apart, perhaps a little more for blackcurrants. Mulch around the base in spring and be careful when weeding since many are shallow rooted. Pull up suckers carefully as they form. Various formats are available but standards or semi-standards are probably the easiest because the branches are clear of the ground, making weeding and harvesting simpler. Late autumn or spring is the best time to plant, preparing the soil well and putting in everything but blackcurrants (which can go slightly deeper) level with the old soil mark.

Gooseberries

Home-grown gooseberries are worth the effort. They need potash in winter or spring. Prune in the winter to make an open centre to the plant, to make picking easier and to reduce the chance of mildew. Cooking gooseberries can be picked in late spring or early summer, but leave them longer on the bush to ripen for eating. Mildew can be a problem so keep the bush well ventilated and cut away any branches the moment they begin to look powdery, or plant the resistant strain 'Invicta'. Other diseases include rust, grey mould and honey fungus.

Red- and white currants

Red- and white currants are botanically similar and easy to grow. They fruit on old wood and should be pruned in winter, but they are unfussy and will produce fruit whatever you do to them. Currants should always be picked as bunches rather than individual fruits, starting in early summer although they will not fully ripen until late summer or early autumn. Aphids and leaf blister can affect the plants but are not usually serious.

Blackcurrants

Blackcurrants are different from the other bushes. They are multi-stemmed, more sprawling, and take up more space in the garden unless you choose a compact variety. They need to be planted so the old soil mark on the stems is 5 cm/2 in below the soil level, as this will encourage growth. You should then cut the stems back to one bud above the ground. This will mean you do not get a crop the first year but it will provide a better framework for the bush.

Prune in autumn or winter, keeping the centre open and, since blackcurrants fruit on the previous year's growth, cut away any old or badly growing branches at the same time. Take out one-third of all fruiting stems each year, leaving no branches more than four years old on the plant. Unless you are going to eat blackcurrants immediately, they must be dry when you pick them. They will be ready to pick in summer and, with tougher skins, will keep better than red- and white currants. Mould, aphids and occasionally honey fungus can cause problems.

Herbs

Herbs are often the first edible plants a gardener grows. Anyone can grow herbs in containers in even the smallest space. They are not an isolated plant category but are often defined loosely as plants with culinary or curative properties. Traditional roles as medicines, flavourings, cosmetics and perfumes are all now being revived. Many, like iris, are grown for their flowers, once regarded simply as a bonus, and herbs and flowers may overlap and change roles. Climate change means that many more herbs and spices will grow well in cooler areas.

Since many herbs have Mediterranean origins, it is not surprising that there seem to be only two essential conditions for most of them to thrive – well-drained soil, however poor, and sun. Although traditionally grown in geometrically patterned beds, they grow equally well alongside other flowers, in pots or window boxes. If possible, it is worth having herbs you really need for cooking close at hand for easy access. 'Fresh' herbs from the supermarket are expensive and aren't as good as your own.

When planning, think of sunshine first – herbs grow better and their taste improves as sun heats the essential oils containing the flavouring ingredients, drawing them to the surface of the leaves. Drainage can be improved by digging grit, sand or organic material into the soil. Many herbs do better when sheltered from strong winds; this explains why traditional planting in walled or hedged gardens or surrounded by little hedges of box is effective.

Herbs are well suited to growing in containers (three or four herbs together) and often go well with other plants. You can move them indoors for shelter from winter cold and wet. Put stones at the bottom of the container and grit in the soil to improve the drainage. Feed them about once a month with liquid feed and keep them well trimmed to prevent them becoming leggy. Many die in winter but some will survive in a pot on a sunny windowsill (French tarragon, parsley, mint and chives, for example).

table 9.3 herbs: planting and care

Herb	Type	Position
Basil (*Ocimum basilicum*)	Tender annual	Sun, poor soil
Bay (*Laurus nobilis*)	Tree	Full sun and protect from frost
Bergamot (*Monarda didyma*)	Perennial	Moist and okay in shade
Borage (*Borago officinalis*)	Hardy annual	Sun and well-drained soil
Chamomile (*Chamaemelum nobile*)	Perennial	Sheltered position with sun and well-drained soil
Chervil (*Anthriscus cerefolium*)	Hardy annual	Semi-shade and moist soil
Chives (*Allium schoenoprasum*)	Hardy perennial bulb	Rich soil and best in sun
Coriander (*Coriandrum sativum*)	Hardy annual	Full sun and well-drained soil
Dill (*Anethum graveolens*)	Hardy annual	Full sun and poor soil
Fennel (*Foeniculum vulgare*)	Perennial	Full sun and well-drained soil
Feverfew (*Tanacetum parthenium*)	Perennial	Full sun and well-drained soil
Lavender (*Lavandula*) (various species)	Shrub	Full sun and well-drained soil
Lovage (*Levisticum officinale*)	Perennial	Sun or semi-shade in rich well-drained soil
Marjoram (*Origanum majorana*)	Half-hardy perennial often best grown as an annual	Full sun and well-drained soil

Mint (*Mentha)* (various species)	Perennial	Sun or moist shade
Oregano (*Origanum*) (various species)	Perennial	Full sun and poor soil
Parsley (*Petroselinum crispum*)	Hardy biennial	Sun or semi-shade in moist soil
Rosemary (*Rosmarinus officinalis*)	Shrub	Full sun and well-drained soil, sheltered position
Sage (*Salvia*) (various species)	Shrub	Full sun and well-drained soil
Tarragon (*Artemisia dracunculus*)	Perennial	Full sun and well-drained soil
Thyme (*Thymus*) (various species)	Shrub	Full sun and well-drained soil, loving drought conditions

10 seasonal reminders

In this chapter you will learn:

- **what you should be doing when**
- **times to work and times to sit back and relax.**

Introduction

The timings given here are deliberately vague as much depends on the weather at any particular time. Follow the guidelines roughly but use your common sense and instinct as well!

Spring

General

New growth appears and days lengthen but frosts and cold can still damage the garden. A good guideline is that if the soil sticks to your boots, it is too wet to work or plant in. Weed, then mulch. Water as necessary. Train climbers.

Shrubs

Plant deciduous and evergreen trees, shrubs and climbers. Prune roses, late-flowering shrubs, late-flowering clematis and spring-flowering shrubs when they have finished flowering. Deadhead hydrangeas.

Perennials

Plant or divide perennials. Stake tall ones. Sow hardy annuals in situ. In late spring give Chelsea Chop to late-flowering perennials (see Chapter 05).

Annuals

Plant out hardy annuals. Sow half-hardies. Plant containers for summer.

Bulbs

Divide snowdrops. Deadhead spring bulbs and feed but leave foliage. Plant summer bulbs.

Lawns

Cut lawn on highest mower setting when dry. Rake and aerate if necessary.

Kitchen garden

Plant potatoes and onions. Sow carrots, lettuce, spinach, peas and beans and continue sowing vegetables for a staggered harvest. Earth up potatoes, stake peas and beans. Sow frost-tender vegetables such as tomatoes, courgettes and cucumbers indoors.

Summer

General

Appreciate the garden, sit out and admire it! Take note of what has done well. All danger of frost is now over. Water as necessary, ensuring the water reaches the roots and does not evaporate off the leaves. Weed and stake plants as necessary. Deadhead annuals, perennials and roses.

Shrubs

Prune spring-flowering shrubs. Trim lavender. Prune wisteria. Trim deciduous and evergreen hedges. Tie in climbers, especially roses, as they put out new shoots.

Perennials

Cut back early perennials and herbs to encourage new growth.

Annuals

Plant out tender annuals. Sow biennials for next year. Give annuals and containers supplement, such as tomato food, to encourage flowers.

Bulbs

Cut back the foliage of daffodils and tulips. Plant autumn bulbs.

Lawns

Leave the lawn slightly longer in case it is very dry.

Kitchen garden

Plant outdoor tomatoes, courgettes, etc. now the danger of frost has passed. Thin out apples, pears and plums as necessary. Prune trained fruit trees, plums and cherries. Continue sowing salad crops. Trim herbs, earth up potatoes, sow salad crops, feed tomatoes.

Autumn

General

You may still need to water, but there can also be early frosts. All plants that are not fully hardy and terracotta pots should be protected as necessary. Check water features for ice and protect outdoor taps. Clear up fallen leaves, especially on lawns. Mulch flowerbeds. Dig any areas of bare soil. Ensure fences and trellis are in good repair.

Shrubs

Plant deciduous trees, shrubs and roses. Check stakes and ties are secure on all trees, shrubs and climbers. Trim hedges, and prune roses and shrubs to prevent damage by wind.

Perennials

Plant or divide if necessary. Cut back perennials after flowering and protect half-hardy crowns with straw. Deadhead unless you want seed heads.

Annuals

Sow hardy annuals. Deadhead until frosts then clear annual bedding plants as they die off.

Bulbs

Plant spring bulbs.

Lawns

Cut grass, but do not cut too short. Feed, rake and aerate if necessary. Sow seed.

Kitchen garden

Dig vegetable garden roughly. Winter frosts will break up the soil.

Winter

General

Look at the structure of the garden and plan any changes. Study seed catalogues and order seeds. Clean tools and tidy the shed. Ensure containers are not sodden or bone dry. Do not be misled by mild days. Water features, lawns, terracotta pots and tender plants are all still at risk from harsh frosts. Dig areas to be cultivated. Sweep leaves.

Shrubs

Plant roses and deciduous trees and shrubs if mild. Plant bare-rooted trees and shrubs. Prune roses and winter jasmine after flowering, also ivy and summer-flowering shrubs. Clear snow off plants, especially evergreens.

Perennials

Start sowing perennial seeds.

Annuals

Sow hardy annual seeds.

Bulbs

Plant tulips. Enjoy bulbs as they begin to appear.

Lawns

Avoid walking on wet or frozen grass.

Kitchen garden

Put potatoes in boxes to chit. Sow broad beans, peas (cover with fleece) and spinach. Prune apples and pears but not plums and cherries.

glossary

acid Soil with a pH of less than 7.

aerate Loosen the soil to allow more air into it, usually by spiking.

alkaline Soil with a pH of more than 7.

alpine A plant that naturally occurs above the tree line. Horticulturally it refers to plants that can be grown in rock gardens.

annual A plant that completes its life cycle (germination, flowering, producing seeds and dying) within one year.

bare-rooted Plants sold without soil around their roots.

bedding plants Flowers that are planted out when almost mature to create a temporary display. Usually annuals, but can include biennials and perennials.

biennial A plant whose life cycle is spread over two years. In the first year it produces leaf growth; in the second year it produces flowers and seeds and then dies.

biodegradable Natural material that will break down organically.

bolting When plants, particularly vegetables, produce flowers and seeds prematurely, often due to drought or poor soil.

bulb An underground stem that has modified to act as a storage organ. Usually consists of layers of scale leaves.

chit Putting potatoes in single layers in seed trays or egg boxes and leaving them somewhere cool and light so they develop strong, green sprouts to grow from.

collar The point where the roots meet the stem (also called 'neck') or on a tree where a main branch meets the trunk or a smaller branch meets a main one.

compost Organic material created when vegetable and plant waste rot down. Also specialized growing mixtures available for particular situations, for example, seeds, cuttings and containers.

cordon Plant (usually fruit tree) pruned and trained to a single stem. Double or U cordons have two stems.

corm Underground swollen stem or stem base. After flowering the old corm withers and a new one develops from it.

crown The point on herbaceous plants where the stems meet the roots and new shoots are produced. Also the upper branched part of a tree.

cultivar Variation of a plant produced by cultivation rather than occurring naturally in the wild. The characteristics will be retained when the plant is propagated.

cutting A piece of stem, root or leaf that can be used for propagation.

deciduous A tree or shrub that loses its leaves at the end of one growing season and re-grows them at the beginning of the next.

division Splitting a plant into several smaller parts, each with roots and shoots, which will then re-grow.

dormancy Period when growth slows down or stops, usually in winter.

drill Narrow, straight, shallow furrow in the soil for planting seeds or seedlings.

ericaceous Plants that will not tolerate lime in the soil and need a pH of 6.5 or less. Also used to describe compost in which these plants could grow.

espallier Plant (often a fruit tree) trained flat against wires or a wall with a vertical stem and tiers of branches running off horizontally.

evergreen A tree or shrub that retains its leaves throughout the year.

family Plant classification of a group of related genera. Not usually given on horticultural labels.

foliar feed Fertilizer applied to the leaves.

form/forma A smaller group of plants within a species, below subspecies and variety. Abbreviation: f.

genus Plant classification in between family and species. Based on the plant's botanical characteristics and indicated by its first Latin name. Plural: genera.

germination Stage at which a seed becomes a plant.

grafting Propagating by artificially joining one part of a plant to another.

ground-cover Plants that are usually low growing and spread quickly to cover bare soil and suppress weeds.

half-hardy Plants from warm climates that may need protection during winter in temperate areas. Usually tougher than tender plants.

hardening off Adapting indoor grown plants to life outdoors. You put the plants out by day and bring them in at night, gradually extending the time spent outside over a period of a couple of weeks.

hardy Plants able to survive year-round outdoor conditions, including frost, without protection.

heel in Temporary planting until the plant can be put in its final position.

herbaceous Plant that does not have a woody stem. Usually dies back in winter.

humus Decayed organic matter that is vital for fertile soil.

hybrid Offspring of plants of two different species or genera.

layering Method of propagation whereby a shoot grows its own root system and can then be cut from the main plant to produce a separate plant. Self-layering occurs naturally.

loam In many ways the ideal soil – easily worked, rich in humus and made up of equal parts of sand, silt and clay.

macroclimate Prevalent climate of the area.

microclimate Climatic variations within a small area. This could be one side of a hill, an entire garden or an area within the garden.

mulch Layer of material placed on top of the soil to conserve moisture, suppress weeds and, in some cases, enrich the soil. May be organic (manure, bark, compost) or inorganic (black polythene or gravel).

neck *See* collar.

nutrients Minerals that are necessary in the soil for plant growth. The main ones are nitrogen, potassium and phosphorus.

organic Substances with plant or animal origins, i.e. containing carbon. Also a method of gardening or farming that does not use synthetic or non-organic materials.

organic matter Natural material that can be used as a soil improver or mulch such as farmyard manure, garden compost or composted straw.

perennial Plant that lives for more than three seasons.

pH Refers to the acidity or alkalinity of the soil. pH7 is neutral, above is alkaline, below is acid.

pinch out Remove the growing tip of a plant to encourage it to bush out.

pollination The transfer of pollen to stigma. Often carried by insects or the wind.

prick out Transfer seedlings from the container they germinated into a larger one.

propagation Making new plants from seeds, cutting, layering or division.

pruning Cutting back plants to reduce size, control shape or to increase flowering and fruiting.

rhizome Fleshy stem that grows underground and acts as a storage organ, producing roots and shoots.

rootstock Plant used to provide a root system for another plant that is grafted onto it. Often used for fruit trees so they will grow to a predetermined height.

seedbed Level area of well-prepared soil set aside for sowing seeds.

seedling Young plant that has grown from seed.

shrub Woody-stemmed perennial plant. Usually branches out near the base with no single trunk.

species Category of classification below genus, consisting of closely related plants. Abbreviation: sp; plural: spp.

spit Depth of a spade's blade.

standard Tree with 2 m/6 ft or shrub with 1–1.2 m/3–4 ft of clear stem below the first branches.

subsoil Layers below the topsoil. Usually less fertile and of poorer texture.

subspecies Subdivision of species; can be further divided into individual varieties. Abbreviation: subsp. or ssp.; plural: subspp.

sustainable A product or activity that does not harm the environment.

taproot Main root that grows down into the soil from the stem. Can become large and fleshy and have other roots branching off it.

tender Liable to be killed or damaged by cold weather or frost.

tines The prongs of a fork or rake.

topiary Creating shapes by clipping and training trees or shrubs.

topsoil Top layer of soil, usually fertile. Depth can vary greatly.

tuber Swollen underground root or stem used to store food.

variegated Leaves marked with patches of another colour, most commonly cream, white or yellow.

variety A smaller group of plants within a species, below subspecies. Abbreviation: var.

Further reading

Plant encyclopaedias

Hessayon, Dr D. G., *The Expert Series*. The volumes on flowers, trees and shrubs and kitchen gardening are particularly useful.

Reader's Digest, *Reader's Digest New Encyclopaedia of Plants and Flowers*.

The Royal Horticultural Society has a series of small and useful plant guides published by Dorling Kindersley. They include *The Good Plant Guide* and *Plants for Places*.

Water features

Archer-Wills, A., *The Water Gardener*, Frances Lincoln.

Wildlife

Baines, C., *How to Make a Wildlife Garden*, Frances Lincoln.

Verner, Y., *Creating a Flower Meadow*, Green Books.

Kitchen gardens

Baker, H., *Growing Fruit*, Mitchell Beazley.

Pollock, M., *RHS Fruit and Vegetable Gardening*, Dorling Kindersley.

Raven, S., *The Great Vegetable Plot*, BBC Books.

Propagation

Cushnie, J., *How to Propagate*, Kyle Cathie.

Plants

A large range of books exists on individual plants, from small pamphlets to multi-volume works. If you become interested in a particular plant it is worth visiting a specialist bookshop or library to find out what is available. You may also find gardens that specialize in that particular plant.

Klein, C., *Plant Personalities*, Cassell Illustrated.

Pavord, A., *Plant Partners*, Dorling Kindersley.

RHS Plant Finder. An annual publication that tell you where you can buy every garden plant you can imagine. Incredibly useful if you want anything out of the ordinary.

General authors

The following is a selection of gardening writers who have produced highly accessible gardening books. They are all individual in style and approach, and if you like one book by a particular author, you will probably enjoy any others that he or she has written.

Marylyn Abbott, Val Bourne, Beth Chatto, Helen Dillon, Monty Don, Penelope Hobhouse, Gertrude Jekyll, Christopher Lloyd, Mirabel Osler, Sarah Raven, Graham Stuart Thomas, Rosemary Verey.

Gardens to visit in the UK

The Royal Horticultural Society: A gardening charity with four gardens in England that are well worth visiting: Wisley in Surrey, Rosemoor in Devon, Hyde Hall in Essex and Harlow Carr in North Yorkshire. The society also runs courses and will give advice on plants and all aspects of gardening.

The National Trust: Runs many important gardens. A yearly guide gives details and opening times. There is a Scottish National Trust.

The National Garden Scheme: This is a charity that organizes garden open days. These are listed in *The Yellow Book*, published each year in early spring. There is a separate scheme and book for Scotland.

The Good Gardens Guide: This is a yearly publication that gives details of the most important gardens open to the public, including selections from the National Trust and the National Garden Scheme. It covers the whole of Britain.

The Good Parks Guide: This is a similar guide to the above, covering parks, many of which are more inspired than you might imagine!

These publications refer to British gardens, but most countries have equivalent organizations and guides. Tourist offices or the internet are good sources of information.

Websites

There is a great number of gardening related sites on the internet, ranging from those devoted to individual plants or gardens to large commercial websites. Many gardens and nurseries have their own sites. Below are a few general sites:

www.rhs.org.uk Royal Horticultural Society

www.gardenorganic.org.uk Henry Doubleday Research Association

www.ahs.org American Horticultural Society

www.gardenersworld.com BBC Gardeners World

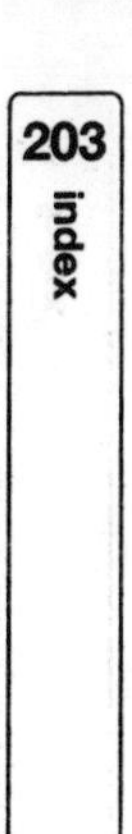

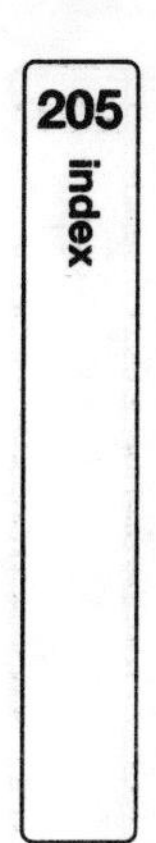